For the four ladies in my life—

Mary Beth, Catherine, Elizabeth and Paige

All finite things reveal infinitude

—Theodore Roethke
"The Far Field"

Foxing at the Edges

The Literary Pretensions of
an Aging Bibliophile

Gregory Thomas

Published by Windsprint Press,
3421 Gladstone Boulevard, Kansas City, Missouri 64113;
windsprintbook @aol.com.

ISBN-10: 0-9629243-3-4

Lay out: Damian Georgiev
Illustrations: Christopher Thomas

First printing: 2009

What Was I Reading? What Was I Thinking?

For at least the last 25 years, with rare exceptions, I have logged at least 100,000 miles per year on airplanes. Some of this has been through international travel, but most of it has been through two- and three-hour domestic flights, frequently shoehorned into a seat in an economy cabin that is not large enough to accommodate an average 11-year-old, much less anything resembling a full-sized adult. I remember when I began flying regularly (five or six times a year) as a freshman in college more than 36 years ago, that a fair-sized person could, on an old Boeing 707, sit in a window seat in coach, get up to go to the lavatory and not cause anyone else in the row to move, much less stand up to let them out.

One consequence of these compressed conditions is that doing much in the way of work on an airplane is precluded for anyone except those who deal almost exclusively with numbers that can be manipulated on a laptop computer or who have several extra pairs of hands with which to juggle documents. In any event, I am convinced that 90-plus percent of the road warriors who immediately pull out their laptops as soon as the 10,000-foot bell sounds are really playing patience or brick breakers or some other game.

As a result of my constant flying and more and more crowded conditions, I read a lot of books. And one of my many failings is that I am almost incapable of doing what is known as "reading a book purely for pleasure or entertainment." For example, I have not read *The Da Vinci Code*, nor have I read a novel by Tom Clancy, Ken Follet, or John Grisham (actually, some of the reviews of Grisham's new stuff wherein he takes on plaintiff's lawyers, formerly the mainstay of his heroes, sound interesting, and I greatly admire him for his support of the Oxford Conference for the Book held at Ole Miss every spring). I generally do not read mysteries and try in most instances to avoid self-help books, quite properly viewing them as only helping the pocketbook of the author and the publisher.

All this time I have had an urge to put some kind of outline around my reading, to make it less random. The objective, to put it another way, was to take on the "world's body," as poet and critic John Crowe Ransom referred to it. To this end, nearly a decade ago, I began at year-end to prepare a list of 52 books that I would read in the coming year—an average of a book per week. I have never made it through more than 30 books in a given year. I did, however, after the first year begin mailing my list to a small group of friends. Some of these passed the list along to other friends, and I found myself over time with a larger group and then found myself not only circulating next year's list, but also enclosing a brief report on what I had managed to get through in the preceding one. Later, this began to take the form of a short memo on what I thought about two or three of the books that had most impressed me.

About the same time, I became concerned about my reading habits. Although I had, over the years, intentionally slowed down as I read things so as to not race over what appeared to be superfluous paragraphs and had tried to think critically about what I was reading, I nevertheless found more and more often that I could report that a certain book had given me pleasure, but six weeks or six months later I could not tell you why.

The other aspect of my reading that troubled me was its lack of focus, other than on making me a better reader. That made me think back to a luncheon I had in 1991 with the late Harry McCall, Jr. Mr. McCall (I never called him anything else, although he was known to his intimates as Bud) gave me my first job. When I heard years later that he had fully retired from his law firm at the age of 75, I wrote him a letter to thank him for what he had done for me. He wrote back to invite me to lunch should I pass back through New Orleans. Thus, I found myself sitting across from him at the Petroleum Club in New Orleans on a gray, dreary November day (the month of his 76th birthday), a man, who as best I could tell had aged very little in the 15 or so years since I had first met him. When I asked what he was doing in retirement (for the tradition in that firm had been that you worked until you were carried out horizontally), he told me that he had been forced to give up tennis because of his knees. He then added, "But there are so many books I have not yet read."

In saying that, he reminded me of something I had forgotten about him. He was never without a book to read. In his 60s, when it would be expected that the managing partner of one of the city's largest law firms would only show up to court on major occasions, he would regularly attend to argue basic motions on behalf of his beloved longtime corporate clients (mostly railroads), sitting for extended periods waiting for his case to be called. And he always had a book with him. Mr. McCall was possessed of a prewar Ivy League education (Princeton, '36), a distinction he deemed important, and the way he carried himself, both physically and intellectually, set an example that harkened back to an earlier time—a time when an education was to provide, as William Alexander Percy wrote, strength of character and delight of mind. It also provided, I think, a framework for continuing to learn for the rest of one's life.

The second influence was a book I read nearly 10 years ago by *The New Yorker* movie critic David Denby, wherein he returned to Columbia University some decades after having gone through the core freshman curriculum (a type of great-books approach) to do it again and see what he got from it this time. The results are a journey to the roots of a liberal education and why it is important. More about that follows.

Thinking back though, there were earlier and perhaps more easily identifiable reasons that I cannot sit on an airplane or put myself to sleep (sometimes a distinction without a difference) with an international intrigue thriller or a simple mystery. That is not to denigrate those forms; after all, two of my favorite writers engaged in each: Truman Capote, having written the script for Beat the Devil, and G.K. Chesterton, being more famous for the Father Brown detective stories than for his other writings. The fact is that my parents were, and my mother remains, omnivorous, if undisciplined, readers. Our town when I was growing up had a more than adequate public library where a very large, school-marmish woman oversaw what I checked out (requiring a note from my mother to allow me when I was 11 or so to check out Irving Stone's novel-cum-biography of Vincent Van Gogh, *Lust For Life*).

The first attempt at imposing order on the natural disorder of my love of books did not really occur until my senior year in high school. This is not to dismiss in any way the many fine English teachers I had up to that time (put aside my complaint that the public schools I attended put no emphasis on the rules of grammar, an omission that crippled me for 20 years afterward and haunts me to this day). The person in whom this new potentiality to communicate was vested was one of my senior-year English teachers, Richard Bushong. Mr. Bushong was a graduate of Olivet College in Michigan and was alleged to be a no-nonsense teacher. He was, in fact, a dedicated teacher and a critical reader in the way that I would later learn that Robert Penn Warren and Cleanth

Brooks meant that term. In a senior year divided into quarters, I took three classes from him, one on creative writing, one on poetry, and one a high school–level introduction to philosophy. It was there that I learned that for a teacher to succeed in demanding the best of his students, all he needed to do was perform the impossible, which was to set the imagination of the student on fire. Mr. Bushong (whom my best friend, Jim Howell, and I took to referring to as Red Elf because of the prominent red moustache he wore) cared deeply about many things related to the written word. He showed me his copy of the collected poems of T.S. Eliot from a course he had taken in college. Every page was covered with marginalia, and he proudly proclaimed that he had more words written in the volume than Eliot did.

What I think he tried to teach us were only a few, but vital, ideas. "What is a poem?" seems today a quintessentially '60s question. But in the fall of 1969, I had been told as recently as two years before by a very young substitute teacher that Bob Dylan was the greatest poet of the 20th century and "Mr. Tambourine Man" the greatest poem ever written (had I had the skill of a practiced wag in those days, I would have asked "Do you mean in English?"). In Mr. Bushong's class we examined all sorts of things, and the conclusion was inescapable that lyrics might be poetry but were not necessarily so. Form, meter, structure, and purpose all became words that suddenly meant something. In their nascent form, they could be both rewarding and dangerous, taking me into a territory of making pronouncements on things for which I had way too little learning and no wisdom at all. But at the same time, it was a taste of the joy in looking at the written word and suddenly saying, "Aha! I understand!"

It was another three or four years before I had another such epiphany. My undergraduate career at Tulane, which was mostly spent studying history and not literature, was suddenly and irrevocably altered by a class I signed up for because the class I wanted was full. The class that I had wanted to take was a graduate-level creative writing seminar taught by Professor John Husband, an older man with a long, white beard that made him look like a character out of Melville. Although I did manage to get into this class in the spring semester, there was nothing transforming about it. It was more a source of amusement watching the six or seven graduate students vie with one another to hold center stage.

The substitute class I signed up for on a whim was Literary Criticism, taught by Assistant Professor of English Richard John Finneran. Finneran was well known to me and most of my friends, not as a man of letters, but because he was a ubiquitous presence on campus, seen on the weekends in the University Center wearing white tennis clothes (which were, even at that advanced date of 1973, still nominally required to use the Newcomb College courts), smoking a curved briar pipe, drinking coffee, and reading. We knew about him because one of our friends was dating another English professor with whom he was friendly. In my sophomore year, Marilyn Burrus, a girl of whom I was very fond, pointed him out to me and said, "That is Dr. Finneran. I have a *crunch* on him." And I had met him once, at a cocktail party off campus in honor of the poet James Dickey, who was speaking at school that night as part of a speaker's program with which I was involved. I did not get to talk with Finneran then because I was summoned to assist Hodding Carter III, who was to act as moderator that night, in pulling Dickey, who was roaring drunk, off a female student, and thereafter babysit him for the rest of the party. We talked about Truman Capote and W.H. Auden and all the other "great queer writers," as he put it, and ended by trading quatrains of Auden's

"In Memory of W.B. Yeats."

Finneran's class was originally to be held in the basement of Newcomb Hall in a classroom that turned out to be too big-there were only eight of us signed up for the course. We moved to a conference room where we sat around a conference table, although Finneran lectured standing up.

And what lectures they were! The textbook naturally began with Plato and Aristotle, which I had superficially read in at least three philosophy courses. But now they had to be applied to something, a measuring stick that would be created, assimilating those first two pillars of philosophy down through Samuel Johnson, William Blake, Samuel Taylor Coleridge, Matthew Arnold, and on to T.S. Eliot, the New Criticism, Northrop Frye (whom we learned was also the speed-typing champion of Canada), and F.R. Leavis, who made the study of literature *a qua* at Cambridge a norm. There was a little bit of Lionel Trilling, but even as a native of the Bronx, Finneran was first and foremost a Yeats scholar (He would go on to be general editor of the collected works of Yeats on which he labored until his tragic and untimely death in late 2005.) and was not in the thrall of the New York intellectuals. I don't remember Alfred Kazin's name ever being mentioned.

What he did manage to inculcate in us was a sense of different measuring sticks: Aristotle and Plato—the classics; Samuel Johnson and the Enlightenment; Coleridge, Blake, and Wordsworth on romanticism; and most of all Eliot and Pound and Yeats, who was a critic as well, on modernism. That is what he communicated in class, but Richard and I rapidly became friends, and it is difficult in retrospect to demarcate where classroom instruction ended and the instruction I received over coffee and in various bars in Uptown New Orleans began. It was here that I learned the elements of Yeats's poetry and the massive tapestry that is his work, encompassing as it does his passion for Maude Gonne, the cause of Irish independence, occultism, and the change that was wrought in his work as a result of meeting Ezra Pound in 1913. Oddly, and this was in class, Finneran also told us that the greatest love poem in the English language was by the most self-indulgent of modern American poets: e.e. cummings and his "somewhere i have never traveled, gladly beyond."

My instruction by Finneran continued through three years of law school. I assisted him by typing one of the chapters of the book he edited on the state of research in Anglo-Irish literature (the chapter by the late Helmut Gerber on George Moore). But being in law school, my outside reading was somewhat restricted (although probably not as restricted as it should have been).

After law school, in the weeks that turned into a couple of months that I spent looking for my first job, I had many hours at home, typing and posting resumes, making telephone calls. But that could only fill a certain number of hours of the day. I was married and my wife, Mary Beth, was at work, and I was I guess bored (and being broke, there was a limited number of ways to relieve the daily boredom). So I plunged into Ayn Rand's *The Fountainhead*. I had read *Atlas Shrugged* while in high school and was told by Mr. Russell, my history teacher, that Ayn Rand made you feel great and powerful for a few days, but then it wore off and you realized it was all nonsense.

Although there are serious flaws in Ayn Rand's so-called objectivist philosophy, the least of which is not, it seems to me, her essential denial of the transcendence of a human spirit capable of sacrifice, her ability to capture the triumph of that spirit is great indeed. I went out into the real world (Finneran's term for anything outside the academy) ready to slay the dragon. Books had enchanted me before, mesmerized me, but this was the first time I felt that a book had, to some extent, transformed me.

In the years that immediately followed, I was like any other young lawyer, mostly too tired and bleary eyed from looking at law books for 10 or 12 hours a day to do much elective reading when I got home. But gradually, I got back to reading, mostly in bed at night. It was also at about this time that a marvelous new independent bookstore appeared on Carondelet Street in New Orleans, DeVille Books, owned by one George DeVille who had, I believe, formerly worked for Doubleday. It was here that I found two books that went far beyond the bounds of what I think their authors intended, that is to open a world that education had trained us to look for, but that most of us, because of the press of our daily lives and the predominance of easier forms of entertainment, never pursued.

The first book I found at DeVille was *The Dream of the Golden Mountains* by Malcolm Cowley. It is a history of his literary life in the 1920s and '30s; editing at *The New Republic*; of friends, such as Allen Tate, the radical Waldo Frank, and Granville Hicks; and of the original production of Clifford Odets's play *Waiting for Lefty*. This memoir is partly about lefty politics and is partly literary history and overall is about the evolution in Cowley's recollection of those days. This led me, for whatever reason, to the multiple volumes of a now nearly forgotten critic Van Wyck Brooks. The first of his volumes I read was *New England: Indian Summer*. Suddenly, a half dozen writers came alive for me the way that Hemingway was alive—although for Hemingway it was from his very careful management of his own image as opposed to the way it was with Henry Adams.

The second book, again an item of *belles-lettres*, was Paul Fussell's *Abroad: British Literary Traveling Between the Wars*. This was another book about writers and books, in this case the generation that produced Evelyn Waugh, Graham Greene, and Anthony Powell, not to mention George Orwell or such now largely forgotten but immensely talented writers such as Peter Fleming (the brother of Bond's creator) and Robert Byron. It connected the dots of the early travels and travel writing, such as Waugh's *Remote People* and Greene's *Journey Without Maps*, to the great fiction these writers later produced, such as *Black Mischief* and *The Power and the Glory*. One of my objectives has become to collect a first edition of every book listed in Fussell's bibliography, although as time goes by those volumes become more and more dear in the marketplace, and I confess that I have been able to acquire mostly copies or, say, the first American edition of something like Powell's *What's Become of Waring*.

In all of this began an unarticulated longing to have within my grasp Ransom's "world's body." I would get depressed at how little I knew of that body when I heard something like the BBC radio quiz show *My Word!* The late Frank Muir and his writing partner Dennis Norden were not academics or philosophers. They were scriptwriters for the BBC. Yet, this weekly broadcast fairly dripped with intellect and sophisticated wit. The historian and biographer Lady Antonia Fraser was an occasional panelist. The questions covered a wide range of topics such as definitions of unusual words, witty parsing of Shakespeare or Dryden, and the golden age of 1930s American cinema. How could I have missed so much of this information and still claim to be educated? The fact that I had two degrees that could be posted after my name seemed to belie what was really inside my brain. At first I blamed this on the California school system. I felt that I had faced college both deficient in grammar and woefully ignorant of the Western canon. It seemed I was not taught certain works in college because it was assumed I had been taught those works in high school. This, it seemed to me, was part of the "Hey, whatever . . . have a nice day" ethos of California education in the 1960s.

Clearly, I would have benefited from stricter instruction in grammar, syntax, diction, and the like. California schools in the '60s were all about students "expressing" themselves without the suffocating restrictions of those things that create a common language among us. As much as I benefited from the somewhat free-form structure of my classes in high school, it is at least arguable that I would have benefited more from reading a supervised version of the classics and having the principles of clear and concise writing (*à la* E.B. White) beat into me.

This was a good excuse, but it was mostly wrong. On the whole there is not time in four years of high school or four years of college to do much more than dip a toe into the vast waters of the canon. It is the purpose of a formal education, I think, to teach you to teach yourself. If you are fortunate, this includes the ability to invoke a discipline to learn about not just the things that instantly amuse you or read only things that are entertaining, but also to occasionally force yourself into some kind of *terra incognita*.

It was thus that I began to try to set out a program for myself by making lists of books that I thought needed to be read. Instead of doing this, I suppose that I could have bought Mortimer Adler's 100 great books, a list he compiled years ago for the Encyclopedia Britannica. I did pick up old, dusty volumes from the Harvard Classics series in various used bookstores. And as it happened, I did buy and read Mortimer Adler's *How to Read a Book*. Mostly though, I thumbed through old textbooks, read a lot of the *New York Times Book Review*, and began to develop my own theory of what a reading life ought to be.

A reading life could not be just a matter of reading "the great books," because I do not know that there is complete unanimity on what those are. I remember the fatuous Hugh Downs saying or writing that one year he decided to see what all the fuss is about, so within a year he read all 100 great books. Putting aside the fact that I doubt that Erasmus could have absorbed all the great books in such a span of time, I found the statement ridiculous. Perhaps more important, the greats are only part of the story. One cannot take in Homer without trying to take in Greek culture, or to try to understand how such a work has affected almost everything that has come afterward. So what do you do? Is it better to pick a subject, an author, or a book and read everything by or about? Or should one's reading have a certain breadth?

And what about new books? Wading through the massive number of reviews and best-seller lists is almost as depressing as looking at the remainder tables in Barnes & Noble. But clearly, limiting oneself to just "the classics" (whatever the definition) is as limited as declaring to never watch another movie made after 1939. So, out of the boredom perhaps that was part and parcel of having moved to Houston and living alone in a new city (having left my wife and daughters in Montgomery, Alabama) at Christmastime 1997, I prepared a list of 52 books that I wanted to read in the coming year and circulated it to five or six friends. Mostly, I wanted my friend Frank Murphy to see the list because of the ongoing nearly 30-year literary discussion in which we intermittently engaged. Frank had also been a student of Richard Finneran's and has remained a dedicated reader. Our discussions have picked up in frequency and intensity in the last dozen years while we have been attending the Oxford Conference for the Book at the University of Mississippi each spring.

Not long after I issued the first list, I picked up a book not on the list that caught my eye in a used bookstore located on

Shepherd Avenue in the River Oaks section of Houston (it has now, tragically, become a nail parlor). More later about the conundrum of books not on the list, but this particular book was called *Great Books: My Adventures with Homer, Rousseau, Woolf, and Other Indestructible Writers of the Western World* by former *New York Magazine* and current *New Yorker* film critic David Denby.

Denby's premise (in contrast to that of Hugh Downs) was one of trying to revive himself with the underpinnings of his formal education. A graduate of Columbia and its core curriculum, he proposed to go back and retake those freshman courses and record his reaction. The resulting book is not only a meditation on a liberal education and a very literate critic's gloss on important writers, but also something of a road map explaining how exposure to the Western canon shapes the way we look at things. As such it is the perfect balance to E.D. Hirsch, Jr.'s *Cultural Literacy: What Every American Needs to Know* or Allan Bloom's *The Closing of the American Mind*. It was a reminder, going way back to Richard Finneran's Literary Criticism class in 1973, as to why we always begin with Plato.

The other thing that Denby's book did for me was to confirm my suspicion that, even with discipline and hard work, educating oneself in this manner would always be shooting at a moving target. Hugh Downs not withstanding, one doesn't get to read the 100 great books that Mortimer Adler selected years ago for Encyclopedia Britannica and then declare one's self educated. If anything, each minor progression along the path will create more questions than it will answer, suggesting more paths to be taken and an equal or greater number that we must forsake in the process. It also told me that my list needed to balance the old and the new and, just as important, branch off into things I knew nothing about, as vast as that area was (and the late Brother Dave Gardner reminds us that you can't believe in nothing because nothing is vast).

In this regard I have been singularly lucky. In the early part of my career as a lawyer I was exposed at long intervals to senior engineers at Ebasco Services in New York. Although it no longer exists, Ebasco was at that time (depending on how you measured) the first or second largest engineering firm in the world and traced its roots back to the engineering and construction arm of the Electric Bond and Share Co., which in the early days of its founding had been controlled by General Electric and Thomas Edison. These were engineers who had designed and built a substantial number of the nuclear power plants of the 1960s and '70s, many of them educated at places such as Rensselaer Polytechnic, Cooper Union, and Columbia.

What I found in the tedious hours one spends on airplanes traveling to meetings and in the far less tedious hours of drinks and good dinners was that there is an elegance in great engineering the same way there is in great literature or great painting or great music. This led me to such works as Henry Petroski's *Engineers of Dreams: Great Bridge Builders and the Spanning of America*, which is a history of the building of great bridges and how the frontiers of engineering are generally crossed first by catastrophic failure and then the refinement that makes the thing work.

Thus, in my mania of making lists of things to read, I began to include subjects about which I knew little or nothing. What it also meant was that I would wade through books like Stephen Hawking's *A Brief History of Time* with only a vague idea what was being communicated. Similarly, I know very little about the visual arts and have made an effort over the last 10 years or so to read one or two books every year about a painter or sculptor. Last year, I read Robert Hughes's biography of Francisco Goya;

this year it was Hilary Spurling's first volume of two on the life of Henri Matisse. My inability here is not unlike my inability with physics; in the same way that I have not been trained and do not know how to manipulate the equations that underlie physics, I do not have much knowledge of the elements of craftsmanship or the techniques of brushstrokes that explain the evolution of painting. More than these surface techniques, however, I lack, in both science and the visual arts, a grounding in the elements that give rise to the artist's intention. T.S. Eliot might say that this is very much beside the point. Then again, Eliot never strayed very far from the fields he knew best.

In addition to attempting to visit subjects that would at least expose me to things I know nothing about (and making me forever more appreciative of the concept of the college introductory survey course), I wanted to avoid reading too much of any one author. But is that the right thing to do? It is difficult to say that gaining a thorough knowledge of, say, Joseph Conrad or Henry James or William Faulkner, for that matter, is a waste of time. Once again, the balance of time versus the resources available becomes a dilemma. One suspects that it was easier for Erasmus to become the most educated man of his age because there were so few books to choose from.

That argument probably does not cut much ice, but the temptation to engage in inadvertent specialization is probably a function of the now ready availability of all books, making the general reader a dying species. The easy access to all books, the vast array of volumes labeled fiction and literature in any Barnes & Noble store, has by its very existence dispensed with the old-style arbiter of public taste, whether in the form of Clifton Fadiman, Bennett Cerf, Bernard DeVoto, or simply my old nemesis, Brunhilde, our local public librarian. There was always the impetus to pick up something that was not exactly up your alley. Now you can wallow in what you have limited yourself to. That the general reader is a dying species is easily measurable on those Boeing 737s where I spend an inordinate amount of time. I once traveled occasionally with a construction executive who had spent the predominant portion of his career working in the Middle East and as a result spent many long hours on flights between the United States and Riyadh, Saudi Arabia. He developed the not surprising habit of always having two or three paperbacks in his briefcase (along with a carton of Lucky Strikes). But the books were all the same. This was about the time Tom Clancy became popular, but there were not half a dozen Clancy novels in print then. Nevertheless, the only thing my friend read were what could be best described as international intrigue thrillers, a genre that, in movies at least, Pauline Kael claimed had reached the end of the road with the Humphrey Bogart movie *Beat the Devil* and its intentionally indecipherable ending in the script by Truman Capote. I notice this trend in my fellow passengers today and in the racks of books in the airport.

Another portion of my inadvertent education came about as a result of hard drinking in New York City. I would like to say that this means I rubbed elbows at the White Horse Tavern in Greenwich Village with the likes of Norman Mailer or Jack Kerouac, but it doesn't. In the early 1980s, when I was virtually living in New York five days a week, I found that I suffered from insomnia in hotel rooms. Actually, what I think I discovered was that the sugar in booze will put you to sleep at 10 p.m. and wake you up at midnight. The only solace in this phenomenon was my discovery that the bookstores on Fifth Avenue in Midtown in those days generally stayed open until two or three in the morning on weeknights. Much to my surprise, it was not merely a collection of perverts looking at dirty books that frequented these places but rather a pretty fair (or actually above-average) cross section of the reading public.

It was in the Doubleday Bookstore (now sadly, an upscale clothing store) that I discovered that most sacred section of miscellaneous works called *belles-lettres*. These were the books that were usually brief and almost impossible to classify, a place where I found Tom Wolfe's *From Bauhaus to Our House*, which falls somewhere between architectural criticism and social observation but was much more fun than either. I found Malcolm Cowley's next book there, *Flower and Leaf*. It was there also that I picked up from the first stack delivered of Larry McMurtry's *Lonesome Dove* and sat up almost all night reading it.

Another half dozen years later, on a Sunday morning in February in 1992 in Montgomery, Alabama, where we were then living, I was sitting on my back porch reading the *New York Times Book Review*. Winters in the middle south are punctuated with a certain number of days when the weather is fine, and this was such a cloudless day with a high temperature of 60 degrees or so, and nothing could be more pleasurable than a Bloody Mary and the paper. It was here that I saw a small ad for the inaugural Oxford Conference for the Book to be held at the University of Mississippi in April. The idea interested me, and Frank Murphy and I arranged to meet in Memphis and drive down to Oxford. We arrived fairly late in the evening, had an excellent meal at the City Grocery (which remains, I think, the best restaurant in Oxford, although there is a surprising amount of competition). The next morning we walked from the downtown Holiday Inn (right on Faulkner's Courthouse Square) to the first place that appeared to serve breakfast—Smitty's (now replaced by a bar and restaurant) behind Square Books.

It was at Smitty's that we got an idea of what the conference would be about, for along with the University of Alabama tennis team (there was an SEC tournament that weekend as well), we spotted at one table George Plimpton—who was there in celebration of the 50th anniversary of *The Paris Review*—and William Styron. They were there presumably attending at the request of the guest of honor, Willie Morris, whose new book of memoirs *New York Days* was to be published shortly.

That long weekend we also heard Kaye Gibbons read from her new novel *Charms for the Easy Life*. On Sunday morning, Willie Morris read from his new work, which picked up where his book North Toward Home left off in 1967, when, at age 32, he had become the youngest editor in chief of *Harper's Magazine*, which, with the demise (more or less) of *The Saturday Evening Post*, was America's oldest magazine.

Morris had been something of a celebrity in my undergraduate days, partly because educated Southerners (even conservatives) enjoy a certain amount of self-flagellation, but at Tulane, it was also because our writer in residence was the elder Hodding Carter, one of Morris's heroes. We were enchanted by the reading, not knowing the firestorm to come over the author's alleged misremembrances, which could well be chalked up to alcohol or perhaps the fact that the stories one likes to tell take on a life of their own, and, if you tell the embellished version often enough, you come to believe it yourself. This has been somewhat confirmed by Larry L. King's recent book *In Search of Willie Morris: The Mercurial Life of a Legendary Writer and Editor*. But for Frank and me, the weekend of undergraduate-level drinking and discussion, together with the burdens-of-life-removing aspects of a college campus in the spring, let us both leave with a renewed vigor and dedication to writing, ideas, and books.

We have returned most years. I don't think any program has been as good as the first, but the sum of the experiences outweighs any given panel discussion or reading. Perhaps the idea of a day or two dedicated to books and reading is its own reward and keeps us coming back.

It was a few years later, living alone in Houston for a long stretch before Christmas that I wrote down in longhand my first 52-book list for the year in 1998. That first list was mailed to about five friends. With the exception of Mr. Murphy, who found the idea amusing, my friends had either no reaction or thought each list overly ambitious (they were and will remain right).

I was trying to do three things with the list: first to fill in the lacunae in my formal education. An offhand list of those gaps would look something like this:

Greek tragedy
Roman history
John Milton
William Shakespeare
Modern European history
Joseph Conrad
Restoration comedy
Henry James
Modern European literature

My second goal was to take a given subject each year and read as deeply into it as time permitted, an obvious contradiction to my previously stated goal of reading widely. One year this subject was Dante; this year it was limited aspects of the French and French literature. My friend Mr. Murphy talks about picking a subject and then reading everything he can until he has exhausted it. Most recently he has done this with Virginia Woolf. To some extent I have done this with Yeats and to a lesser extent with the rest of the high modernists, a course of study that has an easy starting point with the late Professor Hugh Kenner's book *The Pound Era*. I have also made similar efforts with Faulkner and other Southern writers.

My third and most difficult objective was to maintain some semblance of keeping up in the world of more or less serious letters. I mentioned earlier the breadth of knowledge someone like the late Frank Muir exhibited on BBC radio. But what are the sources for knowing what is new to read? Mine have, of necessity, been limited pretty much to the following: *New York Times Book Review, The New Yorker, National Review, The Economist*, and *The Weekly Standard*. I also subscribe to *Vanity Fair*, which occasionally extracts portions of worthwhile books, some of which I have gone on to read, but I would be less than truthful if I did not admit that I primarily subscribe to it for salacious gossip, pictures of beautiful people, and advertisements that promote conspicuous consumption.

It has also been pointed out to me by Mr. Murphy that too strict an adherence to a list precludes me from the new find. My yearly lists include numerous handwritten additions that are due both to changing course and to having run out of things to read while on a trip and being forced to pick up something new in a bookstore at the airport. Still, so much is a matter of taste and interest and not of any set standards.

It has been the rare occasion when I have given up on a book, even one I truly disliked. I managed to finish the extravagantly opaque *The Island of the Day Before* by Umberto Eco. I did, however, give up on Thomas Pynchon's *Gravity's Rainbow* and regrettably gave up on *Tristram Shandy*: the first because I think

Pynchon makes things intentionally unreadable and the second because it is just simply unreadable.

As my mind wanders over the things I select each year for my list, I try to balance the ancient verities with the modern and the contemporary. Thus we come to the problem of taxonomy and definitions. For example, if modernism has a definition at all (which along with words like *dada* or *deconstruction*, I frequently doubt) it is this: the simultaneous minute dissection of human experience while consciously incorporating all of art that has come before. This is why Yeats combined the mythology of Ireland with that of the East, why there are endnotes to *The Wasteland*, and why Ezra Pound engaged in such esoteric efforts as studying ancient Provencal. In fact, it presents an interesting question: If Pound had liked Petrarch more than Dante, would modernism have gone in an entirely different direction?

Another thing that perplexes me is the issue of rereading things. I have read Fitzgerald's *The Great Gatsby* at least a dozen times, and yet I feel somehow guilty doing so because there is (with regard to Mr. McCall) so much I have not yet read. Nevertheless, I have read all of Proust's *Remembrance of Things Past* (or as is now more fashionable, the literal translation *In Search of Lost Time*) twice. The first time was in the summer of 1975 when the United States Army had deposited me at Fort Eustis, Virginia. That was in the translation started by Scott Moncrieff, which remained the standard for nearly half a century. Other than picking up a gem of a phrase here and there ("the only true paradise is the one we have lost"), it was beyond me. More than 20 years later I read the new edition published by The Modern Library, took careful notes, and enjoyed it immensely, although the "better" translation remains the one by Scott Moncrieff. That exercise also led me to read the next year all 12 novels within Anthony Powell's *A Dance to the Music of*

Time, which was self-consciously modeled on Proust. I have become hopelessly addicted to Powell and therefore have to ration myself. The same is true of the collected works of P.G. Wodehouse, so I limit myself to one book a year and resist the temptation to always make that book *Uncle Fred in the Springtime*. Other books are easier to dip in and out of: John Aubrey's *Brief Lives* or, on a given Saturday morning seeing what Samuel Pepys had to say about that day in say, 1667. Of far more recent vintage, I feel the same way about Michael Korda's book *Another Life: A Memoir of Other People*.

In November of 2006, Christopher Hitchens wrote the review of Gore Vidal's second (and presumably last) volume of memoirs *Point to Point Navigation* in the *New York Times Sunday Book Review*. Beyond being the very model of a book review (the kind collected in Anthony Powell's *Miscellaneous Verdicts*), wherein there is just the right mix of what the book is about and what the reviewer thinks of it, Hitchens used a term to describe Vidal's self-education as "polymathic reading," which in addition to having a nice sound to it, I think it fairly well describes what I strive for, even if I don't always accomplish it. It requires a reevaluation every so often to think about the things of which I am abysmally ignorant. Although that list is very long indeed, mathematics and the natural sciences stand out as well as my shameful lack of fluency in another language. Perhaps there is time left for those. I hope so.

The short essays that follow are, insofar as I am able, presented in the same manner in which they were recorded. For better or worse, they are the reactions of an addled brain during flight. There are a few occasions where I have checked references or sought guidance from other works, but for the most part these trifles are merely reactions of the moment. Thus these are my thoughts on a wide range of things on which I am thoroughly unqualified to comment. Napoleon said, "I am an authority on nothing, but I have opinions on everything."

A House for Mr. Biswas by V.S. Naipaul

Having, up until the time I opened the cover of this book, read only V.S. Naipaul's nonfiction, I was not prepared for the irony and wit that pervades this early work (written between his 28th and 30th years) and so came to the first chapters as something of a dullard.

Mohun Biswas was born the wrong way in the island colony of Trinidad in about 1914, not in the thriving Port of Spain but in the countryside among Indian immigrants whose livelihood was earned in the nearly serflike conditions of the cane fields that eventually evolved to the minimal mercantile world of the island that comes to be dominated by Indians.

A pundit, a sort of prophet, is summoned when Mr. Biswas is born, and his predictions are borne out, including the early death of Mr. Biswas's own father, whose demise had been predicted (albeit obliquely) as well as the life of hardship that will follow.

As in the title, Mr. Biswas is continually trying to free himself from the Tulsi family, and the object of that freedom is a house of his own. Yet each time he manages to break away, some disaster befalls him. He takes over the Tulsi family store in the country and does well until Hari, the pundit, comes to bless it, then things go into a rapid decline, to the point that Seth tells him to go back to Hanuman House and they will do an "insure and burn" on the store. Mr. Biswas eventually gets his share of the take: $75.

After each breakaway, Mr. Biswas is forced to return to the Tulsi fold until finally, because he has some education (he reads Marcus Aurelius and Epictitus constantly, although judging from his loud complaints, it doesn't seem that the lessons of the stoics held much sway), he gets a job as a reporter on a newspaper in Port of Spain. Yet, even in the big city, he is forced to live in a communal Tulsi household. What follows is a succession of funny reporting assignments tempered by the difficulties of Mr. Biswas's economic hardship.

Eventually, after going deeply into debt, he buys a house from a solicitor's clerk. Although he is ripped off in the bargain, it is, at last, his house.

What is so startling about this book is the verbal dexterity that Naipaul shows—almost on a par with P.G. Wodehouse—in the day-to-day activities of his characters and the comedy that resides therein. There is also mordant social observation that is all the more startling for its honesty considering the publication date of 1961. In those days it seemed that third-world characters all lived in an Eden destroyed by the Occident. Yet here is the Tulsi family moving from Hanuman house to an Eden-like place called Green Vale, and then trashing it, like they were dwellers of a modern U.S. housing project.

Here too is one of the Gods, returned to Trinidad from England, where the family has paid for him to become a doctor, resuming his place at the top of the Indian immigrant hierarchy and yet spouting a straight Stalinist line, having become a communist while in England. The other God, having stayed in Trinidad, has married well and owns a chain of movie theaters.

It is in the last quarter of the book that we come to know who the narrator really is, for it is not the omniscient one who only sees through Mr. Biswas's eyes. It is Anand, Mr. Biswas's son, who is V.S. Naipaul, with all the derision a young man still harbors for his father and yet retains more than a small measure of regret for not knowing him better.

And it is at the end, through these final chapters and the epilogue, that we come to see that Mr. Biswas is not just a foolish aspirant who leads with his heart and not his head. He achieves his house, although it never achieves the status of paradise that he had dreamed of. Trinidad is beginning to change, and with that change we begin to see with Mr. Biswas the ephemeral nature of even gaining the house he had always sought.

It is here that one sees Naipaul, as a writer, as a man ahead of his time. Referring to the Community Welfare Department, for which Mr. Biswas works briefly (as a result of writing stories for the newspaper on "destitutes"), and the reason it was abolished, we are told "the department was abolished because it had grown archaic. Thirty or twenty or even ten years before, there would have been people to support it. But the war, the American bases, our awareness of America had given everyone the urge, and many the means, to self-improvement." Odd words indeed when compared to the novel that is its contemporary: *Things Fall Apart*, the quintessential book depicting the third world as an unspoiled Eden.

In the end, Mr. Biswas turns out all right. He has his house; Anand is at school in England; and Savi, the daughter, comes home from school as Mr. Biswas is dying, taking a job at a larger salary than Mr. Biswas could have ever commanded. "How can you not believe in God after this?" he wrote to Anand. Indeed, how can you not?

Naipaul's point of view has never been that of the alienated outsider, but is that of the interested, the curious outsider. In his Nobel Lecture he said "When I became a writer those areas of darkness around me as a child became my subjects." Cut off from

India, deracinated in England, the worlds of his ancestors became his great passion to explain.

.

10 December 2005

The Town by William Faulkner

Seventeen years separate the publication of *The Hamlet* in 1940 and the publication of *The Town*, the second volume of the Snopes trilogy, in 1957. In that interval Faulkner had gone from being largely ignored by the American critical establishment (with notable exceptions), to being the darling of Sartre and Camus in the immediate postwar period, to triumph in Malcolm Cowley's *Portable Faulkner*, which was closely followed by the Nobel Prize.

The distance between *The Hamlet* and *The Town* is more, however, than just the distance between the work of a rural genius and that of America's preeminent man of letters (and I will not engage in the Hemingway–Faulkner debate). No, the difference is actually the opposite of what one might think.

Faulkner says in the third volume that the Snopes trilogy was conceived in 1925, and various permutations of Snopes appear in many other works. The big difference between the first two volumes falls into roughly two equal but utterly different areas: The first is that Faulkner was far more in command of his craft in 1940 than he was in 1957. In *The Hamlet*, the omniscient narrator can carry off the extended sentences that are Faulkner's trademark (indeed, my friend Judge Frank McFadden, who knew Faulkner personally, always refers to "one sentence of two pages that was merely a parenthetical comment") and yet keep track of the narrative flow. In *The Town*, the use of multiple narrators (Gavin Stevens, Chick Mallison [i.e., Charles, Jr.], and V.K. Ratliff) leaves a muddle. And Gavin Stevens is so complex a character that his interior monologue sometimes leads down blind alleys. This would be fine, if I thought that the author wanted to take you there, but I don't.

The second problem is that Flem Snopes remains a

28

thorough-going villain, yet there are moments when he verges on being human (which he does not in *The Hamlet*), and one wonders why those involved—at least one—do not recognize it. Or do they? And here the problem (or perhaps opportunity) of multiple narrators is paramount. For, except for the incident when Mrs. Hait's house burns down, which is related by Gavin Stevens, Flem cares only about money and about ridding Jefferson of less desirable Snopes.

But this is exactly what creates the problem. Flem Snopes is a stick figure, a boogeyman. His wife, Eula Varner Snopes, seems much more flesh and blood in her brief appearances as does even Will Varner, her father, who is in most ways the equal of Flem Snopes in his cupidity.

The distinction I think Faulkner may have tried to make here is between the Varners, who are venal, but nevertheless solid citizens, and the Snopes (perhaps with the exception of Wallstreet Panic Snopes), who are deep down, hard-core white trash for whom the author has the same kind of limitless disdain that William Alexander Percy had for Theodore Bilbo. And I should, of course, be reminded that Wallstreet Panic Snopes was only represented to be the son of I.O. Snopes; his parentage was probably otherwise.

Faulkner seems caught in a dilemma—between acknowledging the nature of upward mobility in American society and the idea of "once a Snopes always a Snopes."

24 December 2005

the Town

Leonardo da Vinci by Kenneth Clark

It is probably impossible for anyone who is not an expert to give any meaningful evaluation of Kenneth Clark's work on Leonardo, particularly in light of the vast amount of research that has taken place since the book's last revision (it was originally published in 1937). What can be evaluated is Clark's ability to give the nonexpert reader the feeling of what a working artist's life was like in the Renaissance. It was a time, as Tom Wolfe might point out, when the object was to please the Prince, not have him pay you to insult him.

What one can take away from the book, and which I suspect has not changed significantly, is how Leonardo fit in with his contemporaries and how his studies in perspective changed painting. My father once remarked that people only went to see the Mona Lisa because it was old, not because it was a particularly good painting (as a matter of full disclosure I should include the discussion he had with my mother about church music, wherein she opined that all great church music was Roman Catholic, to which my father responded, "What about 'The Old Rugged Cross'?" not seeing any need to include such minor Protestant composers as Bach or Handel).

As best I can understand, one of da Vinci's enduring contributions was the creation of depth in paintings with the use of scenic backgrounds, as in the Mona Lisa. This would be in contrast to the rather flat background of Giorgione's *La Tempesta*. It is understandable that my parents would not give much credit to that change. But it turns out that all that scenic background did mean something, because, much more than any painter before him, we are able to see to "the back" of Leonardo's paintings. It is also the time that art finally began—after 600 or 700 years—to diverge from the purely religious on the one hand and the purely commercial portrait on the other.

The book refers to Leonardo's drawings—engineering and otherwise—many of which are housed at Windsor Castle, and Clark pays homage to them. But unlike most of what you read today, Clark is not interested in the man who defined the Renaissance man, the broad-based genius who studied anatomy and designed canals, fortifications, and even flying machines. Clark is, first and last, interested in Leonardo the painter. And I think by restricting his interest thus, he has saved it from becoming easily outdated. There have been and will be more and more verified attributions, as well as the debunking of earlier attributions (plus the whole "was it him or others in his studio?" discussion), but that does not matter so much when your objective, as I believe Clark's was, is to set the painter in the context of his time and show the difference he made.

28 December 2005

I, Claudius by Robert Graves

How much of this story that Robert Graves tells is true? We know that before and during the writing of it, Robert Graves read heavily of Tacitus, Josephus, Suetonias, and others; that he allowed his friend T.E. Lawrence to vet the manuscript for errors and anachronisms. Of Tiberius Claudius we know that he was, in fact, an historian, but that all of his writings are lost.

Among the fascinating aspects of this book is the very clear English sensibility and sensitivity to the class system that spills over into the relations of the Roman aristocracy. Yet, and unless I missed them, there are no obvious digs from the proletariat to ruling class, only a sort of Bertie and Jeeves world in which the most outlandish orders of someone like Lord Emsworth are actually carried out.

If there is a swipe at a modern-day villain, it is against the barbaric Germans. For it is on the frontier fighting them that Claudius's brother (the closest thing in the narrative to a hero) gains his name. And it is Caligula's German bodyguards who are prototype S.S. officers.

Claudius is a great vessel in which to pour much history, which he may or may not have known, even already making exception for the inner thoughts of the leading characters that come to Claudius as the narrator by a variety of means. Claudius is the most pliable of means to a literary end, and Graves makes the most of it. He was an emperor about whom little is known, except that he was the brother of Germanicus, the nephew of the Emperor Tiberius, an historian. He walked with a limp and became Emperor essentially by accident upon the assassination of his nephew Caligula.

That Graves plays this for irony from start to finish is no

surprise, for his was the cynical backward look of the generation of young men who had managed somehow to survive and come home from the First War in 1918. His was not the reverence of Rupert Brooke or "In Flanders Fields" but the leave taking of his autobiography *Good-Bye to All That*. He wrote *I, Claudius* to make money so he could continue to write poetry, and yet the scholar and artist could not be kept quiet.

I, Claudius is both a raucous, ironic ride through Roman history, told by a lame, abused, and cynical Candide and a meditation on why people tolerate the kinds of government they do. Throughout, we are reminded that Augustus only assumed the powers of Emperor as emergency measures in a time of civil war, culminating in the defeat of Antony and Cleopatra at Actium. Year after year it was assumed that someday the republic would be restored, even as Augustus fretted over the designation of an heir to his Empire.

His successor, Tiberius, is clearly the wrong choice. Craven and cowardly, he banishes or executes his enemies—both real and imagined, even unto the murder of his nephew Germanicus-accomplished with the connivance of his mother Livia. Yet after 100 pages or so of Tiberius's outrages, Claudius tells us that except for those being accused of treason and executed, things for the average Roman citizen were going pretty well.

And therein lies the author's message—at least to the extent he would risk ruining a great story by inserting one—that things remain as they are when most of us are comfortable. Rather prescient of the rabble-rouser to the north of him in Germany at the time he was writing this.

Beyond that, the level of daily detail makes Rome live in a way that no epic movie ever could (of course one of the problems with epic movies is crowding battle scenes with more soldiers than probably existed in the entire population of the known world at the time). And unlike in the movies, the houses of Rome were not the stone edifices that look more like the lifeless ruins they would become over the next millennium, rather they were places that were lived in and housed the everyday appurtenances we still recognize. This is also true of the commercial world and the organization of the military—they are worlds both strange and recognizable.

1 January 2006

Heloise and Abelard by James Burge

One has to get past the TV documentary approach of this book (and it is, to some extent, a companion book to a BBC documentary) to enjoy it. Particularly irksome is the author's tendency to explain in oversimplified terms certain aspects of early European history, and one can take exception with his hauling about of terms like Dark Ages and Middle Ages to suit the point he wants to make about the state of education or learning in France in the 11th and 12th centuries. His carelessness with the taxonomy of epochs seems to ignore the point that while, yes, there were monks working away at copying learned texts, that after the fall of Rome and the destruction by fire of the library at Alexandria, most of classical learning was lost until the beginning of the Renaissance. Thus, Abelard, the master of logic, was struggling to recreate concepts already well developed by Plato and Aristotle.

But this is to perhaps criticize a book for failing to achieve goals that it did not set for itself. For absent those criticisms, it assembles the correspondence and gives a fairly smooth, flowing understanding of the lives of the two lovers.

Abelard, taken in his own words, is very full of himself, and Heloise is a saint, a saint whose passion for her lover never dims. Abelard was run out of every religious community in which he lived, a professional malcontent overly impressed by his own erudition and mental powers. Heloise, once she had taken the veil, became the most successful abbess in France. And yet she remained true to her dream of Abelard all the long years after a child, a marriage, and the castration of Abelard. All of these are put into the context of a wonderful love story, despite my earlier criticism and my criticism that the author also has the tendency to judge things in terms of contemporary sensibilities.

The great thing this book accomplishes is to give the genuine feel of a world lighted solely by candles, of a time when the shortest of journeys took days and the fortunate few who could read may have had access to only a handful of books. It was, by our lights, a cruel world, but one whose insularity is a comfort to look back on.

5 February 2006

Travels With My Aunt by Graham Greene

Why does Greene refer to this and a few other works as *entertainments*? Surely they contain all the elements of the so-called Catholic novels: an old world crumbling away, a new world in utter chaos, and the value of faith to sinful yet good people.

The narrator meets his Aunt Augusta for the first time since infancy at his mother's funeral. It is clear from her first appearance that she is a free spirit, attached as she is to a black man named Wordsworth, whom she met when he was the doorman at a cinema. What follows is an improbable trip to Istanbul via the then-decaying Orient Express and the introduction of a true Graham Greene heroine, or semi-leading lady, in the person of Tooley, a young American student. She also is a free spirit, but a nubile one.

There also enters Aunt Augusta's long-lost love, an Italian art dealer wanted by Interpol for dealings during the war, who ultimately ends up in South America, followed by Tooley's father, who may or may not be a CIA agent.

The main points (as the World News of the BBC characterizes such) are the same that Greene makes in *Brighton Rock* or *The End of the Affair*, except with a lighter touch and a happier ending as well as more humor from start to finish. It is the humor that is the difficulty. There are light moments throughout; however, Greene cannot compete with Evelyn Waugh for laughs, and actually is a far distance behind Anthony Powell on that score, too. I believe it was Malcolm Muggeridge who once wrote to Greene saying that he (MM) had spent his life as a sinner trying to be a saint, whereas Greene had always been a saint trying to be a sinner. Waugh's innate wickedness gives us the misdirection that is good for a thousand laughs. Greene can give us only so much, and the reader can feel him becoming squeamish at the indiscretion of his own characters.

Entertainment indeed. It is merely another lesson in disguise.

11 February 2006

A World Without Time by Palle Yourgrau

Anyone lacking the requisite Ph.D. in physics or philosophy might avoid this book, assuming that it will be indecipherable. But this book functions on three distinct levels: It is, first, a testament of the relationship between Albert Einstein and Kurt Gödel, it is an exposition of the intellectual currents in both physics and philosophy (with side trips into mathematics and logic) that drove thought from the fin de siècle to the post–World War II world, and it is finally a critique of intellectual snobbery from the Vienna Circle to the early 21st century Ivy League.

The difficult portions of the book, which the author works at diligently to make accessible, deal with the events that converged at the end of the 19th and beginning of the 20th centuries-specifically dealing with Einstein's special theory of relativity in 1905 juxtaposed with the problems inherent in set theory as demonstrated by Russell's Paradox and later by Gödel's incompleteness theorem, and the further difficulty that quantum mechanics presented to Einstein in his quest for the so-called unified field theory.

Somewhere in this density of words is a discussion of time—Einstein's curved spacetime of the special theory and Gödel's surprising but persuasive thought on the subject takes him back to the very core of being a Platonist. Gödel's conception of time, which is very attractive to my way of thinking, is that it consists of slices, like points on a line that are always there reaching infinitely in either direction.

This belief is so disliked by Cambridge's Lucasian Professor Stephen Hawking, that he put forth what Yourgrau calls an *anti-Gödel amendment*. This is a prelude to the thorough raking over the coals Gödel gets from the academic philosophical establishment, who conclude that he was a brilliant logician but, after all, logic is not physics or philosophy.

The author has an appropriately hostile reaction to this snobbery, but it leaves me torn between two thoughts. The first is that any contribution that arguably advances the fields of ontology and cosmology is *a qua* philosophy. Given that what now passes for philosophy suffers from the sin of being overly focused on intentionally recondite minutiae, it is difficult to understand the criticism. The other aspect goes beyond the dispute between the two sides here and harkens back to Jean-François Revel's remark that philosophy ceased to mean anything when it quit asking the question "How should men live?" Gödel did not pretend to be a systematic philosopher, and how many of those have there been since Kant? Certainly none of Gödel's academic critics arise to that category, and he never took himself to be any more than a piece of the puzzle.

It is in the latter stages of the book that it becomes difficult for the nonspecialist. There is a fair amount of discussion about Wittgenstein and of the limits of language. I have struggled through some of Wittgenstein and read closely Ray Monk's exhaustive biography of him, but have no way of judging if *Tractatus* is the piece of trash Yourgrau says it is.

Interwoven into the technical discussion is the rather sad story of Gödel's life. One can call it tragic perhaps, more than just sad, in the same way that Simone Weil's life was tragic. They were both believers (Gödel, as he said, believed in the God of Liebnitz, not the God of Spinoza, because the God of Spinoza was less human and the God of Liebnitz was more), but they were both unable to take from their believing the joy that is supposed to reside there.

Like Simone Weil, Gödel starved himself to death,

although it took Gödel more than 20 years to do so, roughly from the time of Einstein's death in 1955 to Gödel's in 1978. It was during those two decades that he produced a body of work that is just now, nearly 30 years after his death, being unearthed and evaluated. Again, Yourgrau puts this down to the arrogance and prejudice of the academy. Unlike Wittgenstein, who ultimately rejected all his own earlier work and spent his last years solely focused on tearing down the work of others, Gödel spent his life building on and refining his original theorems. Yourgrau, winking at Anaïs Nin, refers to Gödel as "a spy in the house of logic."

Yourgrau saves his most stinging criticism for the unregenerate, unreconstructed positivists of both the Vienna Circle era and now. He states that they steadfastly refuse to make ontology subservient or even equal to ethics, and as a result "Here is a crucial difference between truth and proof: a mathematical proof . . . is always a proof in, and relative to, a given formal system, whereas truth, as such, is absolute."

It is to Gödel's credit that, even as a specialist, he understands the difference between the two searches, very much consistent with what Revel says. Spinoza's God was less than a person and Liebnitz's more than one. It is in losing sight of the distinction that the search for knowledge has gone astray.

19 February 2006

Henry Adams and the Making of America by Garry Wills

No serious thinker, left or right, questions that Garry Wills is a scholar of the first rank. That his output over the last 10 years has covered an odd assortment of subjects makes him difficult to pigeonhole, but at the same time he takes us happily back to the 19th century and first half of the 20th, when a first-rate mind (one thinks of Carlyle or Shaw or Churchill) was allowed to roam over a multitude of subjects now reserved for specialists.

This book brings to the fore Henry Adams, but not the taciturn and almost bitter Adams of *The Education* (which, I confess, is the only work of his I have read all the way through) but the Adams who was part of the world of Henry and William James, John Hay, Henry Cabot Lodge, and Theodore Roosevelt and Oliver Wendell Holmes, Jr. It is the Adams who is an enthusiast as an historian; it is the Adams who is part of the world described by Louis Menand in his book *The Metaphysical Club*, the world that forms the end of Van Wyck Brooks's volume from 70 years ago *New England: Indian Summer*.

In the process, it is Wills's intention to rediscover the Adams who, far from the "cheap pessimism" of *The Education*, wrote in an epigrammatic style worthy of Voltaire: "and the day when the nation's politics turn exclusively on questions of fidelity to great moral abstractions is a disastrous day for good government."

He wrote that in an essay on American finance published in the *Edinburgh Review* in 1869. He became not an apologist for Adams family politics but the purveyor of an explication of the limited government of Thomas Jefferson as opposed to the Jefferson who engineered the Louisiana Purchase. He does this in his two great histories: *The History of the United States of America During the Administrations of Thomas Jefferson* and *The History of the United States of America During the Administration of James Madison*, each published in eight volumes and taking the young republic from 1800 to the country beyond the War of 1812 into the world of 1816. It is Wills's point to revive an interest in these two works (which are readily available in the Library of America), and he does so by, in the second half of his book, following the chronology of the other two. He quotes from them so extensively that at times what he is providing is essentially continuity between sections of dense (although categorically not unstylish) 19th century prose.

Wills's avowed purpose is to rescue Adams from the darkened corner to which he had been relegated by, among others, the late Richard Hofstadter. He further attributes to Adams a revolution in American historiography by his having been the first to seek out European primary sources (the British Museum and—presumably from his description, although he does not name it—the Recopilación de Los Leyes de los Indios in Madrid). Adams further was the lynchpin in the intellectual reconciliation between North and South after the Civil War, based largely on his friendship with Mississippi Senator Lucius Quintus Lamar.

It is in this regard that Wills, doubtless feeling safe in his judgments, strays from the reporting of New England secessionism or the aspects of geographic nationalism or the various aspects of the Alien and Sedition Acts. He states rather flatly that, although Adams had been an ardent opponent of slavery, he did not favor equal rights for the black man; in other words, his position was exactly the same as Lincoln's. This is doubtless an accurate statement. Where I fear he goes astray is in an all-out attack on those who question presentism in judging someone from the past. Put another way, it seems reasonable enough to say that it is unfair to judge a man's opinions on civil rights (as the term is applied to the Negro Rights movement of the second half of the 20th century) by today's standards of fairness. Wills disagrees with this whole heartedly, and if I understand his argument, it is appealing to the conservative mind because the argument is that there is only one moral right and one moral wrong, and they are unaffected by intellectual or social fashion. That would be and is, in fact, appealing. But it neglects at least two facts. The first is a refutable presumption that civilization, at least in the ultimate turns of the gyre, improves itself. Can we argue that the Roman soldiers who suffered rocks thrown at them by native Britons were no more civilized than their attackers, or that the Britons of 1850 were not more civilized than the Britons of 30 B.C. or even that Roman Legion?

The second argument is just the defense against presentism that Wills deplores: that our forebears made judgments based on the information available to them, which did not include vast arrays of data that are available to us today. It also acknowledges the possibility that under the circumstances, the harsh views of a Henry Adams or of a Douglas MacArthur or a Winston Churchill on a subject about which today we may be hypersensitive might have been not only reasonably arrived at under the circumstances, but also under the circumstances might have been right.

Neither democracy nor civil rights are conferred by a benevolent creator, despite Mr. Jefferson's eloquent statement. They are created by the minds of men whom we hope can handle them.

That quibble aside—and it really isn't a quibble, it is the debating of a close point—Wills's book serves its purpose well.

13 March 2006

Act One by Moss Hart

In the fall of 1930, at the beginning of the second year of the Great Depression, a 25-year-old playwright named Moss Hart, in collaboration with the highly successful George S. Kaufman, had his first play presented on Broadway. *Once in a Lifetime* was a resounding success, and based on his 50 percent of the royalties, he would draw $1,000 a week for the run of the show, which, after the opening night was booked for a year's run at the Music Box Theater. The show's producer was the legendary Sam Harris, partner of George M. Cohan.

This book, published in 1959, is the story of Hart's rise from abject poverty to, at the age of 25, the toast of Broadway. It is a marvelous tale, and Hart, stating the obvious, is a wonderful writer. His insights into himself and his family are the kind of thing one takes down as quotes to carry around for the right occasion. An example is his description of his mother, who spent a fair portion of her life running interference among Hart's grandfather, father, and Aunt Kate, eccentrics who, I think to some extent, populate such plays as *You Can't Take It With You*. Of her he writes "the struggle robbed her of her children—people who spend their lives in appeasing others have little left to give in the way of love."

That is a great quote, but there is so much material like it that the reader comes away feeling Moss Hart was a true precursor to our own self-absorbed generation.

In that regard, a comment made by Kenneth Tynan in an essay about Mel Brooks gives us something of the context. His essay begins at the book party for the publication of *Act One*, where Brooks, better known then as a writer for Sid Caesar, is doing a routine as a Viennese analyst who is being interviewed *à la* his later routine as the 2000 Year Old Man. Tynan remarks offhandedly that it was an appropriate routine because Hart had "famously" been in analysis for more than 20 years.

This only fueled the already rampant speculation that he was homosexual. Although he had married the actress Kitty Carlisle in 1946 (when he was 42) and they had two children, one can (perhaps only having been provided that fact) feel the edge of someone who would like to tell you more, but can't. Today I think you would get the confession—and praise for his being candid-even if it wasn't true. But that is not what this particular book is about. It is about struggle, perseverance, and learning. It is about the world of the theater at the end of the Algonquin Round Table and after the beginning of the Catskill resorts, where Hart worked in the years when he was trying to become a playwright.

And curiously, it is about failure, but not the failure of his first play, *The Beloved Bandit,* which is a rollicking tale. It is, rather, the failure that seems to have hung over his family: his Grandfather who would have led the American Federation of Labor but for a falling out with Samuel L. Gompers; his father, a cigar maker put out of work by a machine, who seems never to have recovered; and of Aunt Kate, who seems to have been an English–Jewish precursor to Blanche DuBois. Then there is the odd complacency—at least from the author's telling of it—of a family that would let someone so young simply assume the responsibility for the care and maintenance of the adults in the household.

Perhaps the most important thing to come from this book is the portrait it gives us of George S. Kaufman, who at first seems to us rather taciturn, certainly not the wit of the Algonquin Round Table. I suspect Hart overplays this for effect, for he does state that if the book has a hero, the hero is George S. Kaufman. Little by little, the Kaufman who dined with Harold Ross, Franklin P. Adams, Dorothy Parker, and Edna Ferber emerges as the wit and raconteur of legend, not to mention the Kaufman who for years carried on a torrid affair with the actress Mary Astor (and that probably wasn't generally known in 1959, and Hart, clearly a man of his generation, certainly doesn't mention it). It allows Kaufman to be the hero when, standing on the stage of the Music Box Theater on opening night, 1930, he announced that "this play is 80 percent Moss Hart."

It is the perfect ending and beginning, and it is too bad Hart did not live to tell us the second act, of writing *You Can't Take It With You* and *The Man Who Came to Dinner.* But we are left with the story of a singular triumph, which nearly 50 years after the writing and more than 75 after the fact, is still thrilling.

21 March 2006

The First World War by John Keegan

The emphasis of this book is first and foremost the battles that were fought, the movement of troops, and the decisions of generals. Only secondarily is it concerned with politicians and political decisions. The only major exceptions to this are the decisions of Kaiser Wilhelm, which stand as bookends. Wilhelm was the man who could have prevented the First World War altogether or ended it at the end of 1914 or beginning of 1915 and who arguably prolonged it from July 1918 to November.

Two things come of what is a clean, precise narrative that intentionally does not digress to tell many of the tales, romantic or otherwise, of the Great War (for example, there is no mention, none, of the Christmas Truce in 1914). The first is a clear idea given to the reader of the placement of armies and second, the chronology of battles.

The lessons to be drawn from the war, Keegan tells us, are not necessarily the ones that so easily come to mind: ossified or sclerotic generals insouciantly sending young men off to their deaths. To be sure, in Joffre and in Sir John French, the inability to lead cavalry charges around the enemy's flank contributed to a stalemate on the Western Front that lasted more or less from September 1914 to the war's end. At the same time, it becomes clear that the technology of entrenchment and the increased range and power of artillery probably contributed as much as anything else to the stalemate. It was only with the advent of the tank that the ability to breach the other side's defenses became a real possibility, and the tanks capable of doing that did not appear until late 1917 or early 1918. By that time, Russia had collapsed and made peace with the Central Powers, and the armies on the Western Front were in a state of exhaustion. The Germans did not know the extent of the French mutiny in the south, or in any event were unable to capitalize on it. Meanwhile, even with the Russian peace, Germany was sliding into an economic sinkhole because of four years of blockade. They additionally miscalculated when, in 1917, they declared unrestricted submarine warfare. America would enter the war and not be distracted by Germany's adventures in Mexico.

Perhaps the most fateful decision was to allow the U.S. troops to act as a separate army rather than as replacements to the French Army (which was what the French wanted). Although Keegan does not speculate, had the French prevailed, it would be easy to see that the war would have dragged on through 1919; although, I think it is also clear that the U.S. fleet added to the British would have maintained a blockade that ultimately would have brought on the German collapse, perhaps before the beginning of 1919.

Perhaps the more interesting "what if" on which to speculate is how the Eastern Front might have turned out differently had the Tsar's armies performed better or had the British and French on the Western Front been able to flank the Germans north and south in the autumn of 1914. Or even if Admiral Fisher had not gone wobbly at Gallipoli, there would have been no sealed train to the Finland Station, and what a different place the world would have been.

Undated

Arthur and George by Julian Barnes

For the first two or three chapters of this book we are not told who Arthur and George are. Having an advance reader's copy of the book, I do not know if the dust jacket on the first edition does so or not. We eventually learn that Arthur is Sir Arthur Conan Doyle, and we are told pretty much the whole story of his life. The same is true of George Edalji, the son of an Indian father and English mother. His father is the vicar of a country parish in the Midlands.

We watch both men grow up—Sir Arthur through a contradictory set of circumstances, containing a somewhat hard-scrabble life in Edinburgh. He had a dipsomaniac father and a dominating mother, but at the same time a Catholic school life that leads to Vienna, then medical studies. He ultimately goes on to become the creator of Sherlock Holmes.

George, by contrast, grows up isolated, held at a distance by his schoolmates because of his mixed-race background. One of those tells George that "he is not the right sort." Ultimately, George is arrested by the local constabulary for a series of animal mutilations. At first, the reader is convinced that George, now a solo solicitor in Birmingham, commuting by train every day and still living in the rectory with his parents, could not have committed the crimes. But Barnes does not quite let him off the hook, so that when he is convicted and sent to jail, the reader retains a certain amount of doubt that he is a victim after all.

Running parallel to this story, in short, alternating chapters, is Conan Doyle's rise to fame as the author of Sherlock Holmes, the invalid state of his first wife, his (mostly) unfulfilled passion for the woman who would become his second wife, and his developing interest in the occult. This dates his interest much earlier than

I had previously read, usually ascribing it to the death of his son in the First World War.

After reading about George's case, Sir Arthur takes it up as his cause, writing editorials and petitioning the Home Office. This is all subsequent to George being given an early release from prison. At the end, as a result of Conan Doyle's intense efforts, George is somewhat exonerated, more so in public opinion than by the Home Office itself. It is not until the Second World War that the real culprit confesses, nearly half a century after the event. Sir Arthur Conan Doyle received no satisfaction from this, having died in 1930.

George stays on in London, returns to practicing as a solicitor, specializing in conveyancing, living out the next 50 years with his sister. He is given to us as a character of ambivalent sexuality, which can perhaps be ascribed (or certainly his seemingly asexual nature) to the isolation of his upbringing. He is a thoughtful if somewhat sad character.

Although in one of the final scenes, Barnes shows us Conan Doyle's widow attending a rally of occultists at the Royal Albert Hall, he does not really remind us how pervasive interest in the subject of the occult was from the late 19th century to the beginning of the Second World War, *vid* the number of societies W.B. Yeats belonged to. Conan Doyle was engaged in something odd, which for its time, it was not.

Still, the book succeeds on several levels, chiefly as a mystery and more so as a meditation on identity. At the end, both Sir Arthur and George are Englishmen.

10 May 2006

A Fable by William Faulkner

This is the third time I have read, or perhaps tried to read, this book. The first was in high school and the words mostly fell under my gaze without making their way to my brain. This time, I feel like I made it through, although I am left with the impression that the second half of the book is better written than the first half (i.e., everything after the story of the stolen racehorse). Perhaps I believe this because Faulkner, not just here but in some other works, has the infuriating habit of not using his characters' names, or in some cases never naming them at all. Is it that he does less of this in the second half, or is the reader more used to this quirk by then?

The bare outline of the story is well known: during Holy Week 1917, a battalion of the French Army mutinies. Faulkner's fictitious mutineers, 13 in all, are a Jesus and his disciples. This is the book famously outlined on the wall of his study at Rowan Oak, but the simple straightforward retelling of the crucifixion exists more tangentially to the story than what is shown in that outline might suggest.

Perhaps once one develops the self-discipline to make it through the digressions, circumlocutions, and intentional opaqueness, which can be more demanding in certain Faulkner stories than in others, two things are found: mordant observation of the human condition and a pondering on the meaning of larger themes. Sometimes, as in *The Town*, the second volume of the Snopes trilogy, Faulkner is able to achieve this goal and give the reader comparatively easy access (even with, or perhaps because of, the use of multiple narrators). Here, more so than in any of his other works I can think of, with perhaps the exception of *Light in August*, it is all density and darkness.

In my dullardness, I also wonder about what might be termed the inevitable horse detour. He does this here and in *The Hamlet*. In *The Reivers*, the horse detour comprises the entire book, as it is in the eponymous story of *The Unvanquished*. Where it comprises the entire book, it is hugely entertaining. In *A Fable*, the story of the stolen racehorse seems not to fit. *A Fable* is more concerned with symbols than any other Faulkner work I know, and I do not see how the improbable story of the stolen racehorse adds to it. This is less true of the story of the hanged man and the bird.

Now, for what does work: the hopelessness of the trenches, the fatalism of the 13, the comings and goings of the generals far behind the lines. And this I think was something Faulkner knew he was capturing. The First World War was the first time the generals, at least in any European war, had been so far removed from the actual fighting.

Christ is easy enough to find, the two Marys as well. But who is the French General? Is he Pilate? For he sits in judgment. Is he Satan? For he offers the Christ figure freedom while they talk on a mountaintop. Is he God? Because he may be the Father. Perhaps in another 10 years I will read this again and make more of it, as I seem to each time.

14 May 2006

Sartre: The Philosopher of the Twentieth Century
by Bernard-Henri Lévy

First, a confession. I have liked the idea of Bernard-Henri Lévy since I first read about him as one of the so-called *nouvelle philosophes* in the late 1970s. A profile of him in *Vanity Fair* several years ago did nothing to diminish his image as a rock star intellectual who also did not happen to be reflexively anti-American. But he is also, like his subject in this book, someone you read more about than you actually read.

If I recall correctly, at the time of Sartre's death (or perhaps it was earlier, during one of his many involvements in some leftist protest) William F. Buckley described him as primarily a superverbalist who wove his philosophy into plays and novels. Buckley treated him as not being a systematic philosopher, which he was not. Perhaps there have been only a few since Kant: Hegel perhaps, maybe Henri Bergson. Ours is, after all, the age of specialization. More important, Sartre was more interested in being a public intellectual, much as Bertrand Russell was in England, than he was in being like Spinoza, spinning a comprehensive philosophy while making a living grinding lenses.

This book is neither a biography in the conventional sense nor an objective study of Sartre's work. In the first place, Lévy himself obtrudes too much into the narrative, not merely as commentator but also as participant, for it to be either of those. He begins by giving us the Sartre (and Simone de Beauvoir) of the headlines. He writes (or perhaps is it translates? I cannot judge) in a present progressive tense that at times becomes an irritatingly bad imitation of Damon Runyon. He goes on to tell us about the traditions from which Sartre broke away. The first and foremost of these traditions was represented by André Gide. For Sartre, he represented the traditional avant-garde (that is my oxymoronic formulation and not Lévy's), which for the young Sartre (as opposed to André Malraux) had reached the desiccated status of effete slumber when compared to being a man of action on the Left. He follows this with a professional break from Martin Heidegger, yet Lévy also contends that he remained a Bergsonian after a fashion, even though in the 1930s that was what all French intellectuals thought they were breaking from. This is all well and good, but Lévy fails to tell us what it is to be a Bergsonian, and most of us do not carry around a user-friendly compendium of Bergson's work. We also have only a limited understanding of what Husserl's theories of phenomenology were and how they related to the thinking of Bertrand Russell or Wittgenstein—the path that philosophy took from the positivists of the Vienna Circle on, as opposed to the road taken by Sartre. The author does not make it easy for the average reader, but that probably was not his intent.

When Lévy addresses the nuts and bolts of Sartre's ontology, it has a certain romance to it, but again, it makes large demands. The problems of cognition, of knowing subject and object, requires one who is at all serious about understanding what he is reading to sit in amid a stack of cross-references while doing so. Midway through, I found myself pulling down Bergson's *Matter and Memory*, two books on Spinoza and cross-checking the *Cambridge Dictionary of Philosophy* on the subjects of Descartes, Husserl, Hegel, and Nietzsche.

The fact that Sartre harkens back to Spinoza's idea of immanence, i.e. that all rules stem from the natural order of things and hence man's natural power of reason does not seem to point us much of anywhere does not seem to square with his emphasis on the individual as a being of conscience in an otherwise inert universe. But then again, neither does his Stalinism. As Lévy points out, although Sartre produced a massive amount of writing, he failed to write two books one would have expected him to. The first is the promised autobiography that doubtless would have been a mega best seller. The other book never written is the ethics, which would have had to somehow harmonize the inconsistencies of his philosophy, which almost acknowledges the God of Spinoza, if not the God of Liebnitz. This was the book he promised at the end of *Being and Nothingness*. It is an entirely personal matter with me, but I quite agree with Jean-François Revel when he wrote to the effect that philosophy went off track when it ceased to ask and answer the question "How should men live?" This is my problem with Sartre, because he simply answers questions with other questions, much the way the existentialist theater of the absurd does. This leaves him free to embrace the worst butchers of history without showing how that meshed with his writings.

Yet none of this is what Sartre is supposed to be about. *The Cambridge Dictionary of Philosophy* defines Sartre as an unabashed Cartesian, whose greatest belief is in freedom and the responsibility that goes with it. To this, those of us who grew up in the '60s can only respond with "huh?" Is this not the man who embraced Mao? Is he not the man who never renounced Stalin and all the associated claptrap of the Popular Front?

Let us fall back on Nietzsche, despite the fact that he probably took all sides on all issues at one time or another. He fairly well describes the fork in the road that Sartre was presented with and which Sartre, much like Yogi Berra, takes.

If the little I understand of Nietzsche is correct, he addressed two major points, the first being a need to escape from the nihilism brought on by modern science and set forth at its most depressing by Arthur Schopenhauer in *The World as Will and Representation*. The second is a massive distrust of the rise of bourgeois society and the rule of the masses. In this sense Nietzsche is very close to Søren Kierkegaard, although Kierkegaard does not declare that "God is dead" but rather makes the leap of faith. In either case, though, the individual is faced with the prospect of filling the void created by the absence of received law and wisdom. Thus, is what Sartre provides us (or Nietzsche) philosophy or merely a statement of social condition?

So we return to the confusion of subjects and objects, of Kant and the *Critique of Pure Reason*, and most of all Descartes. *Cogito ergo sum* becomes not just the subject–object argument focused on consciousness as an activity rather than as a "thing," but is summarized as *pour soi* versus *en soi*, the former being the Cartesian "being for itself."

Given Lévy's public image, it is odd that he defends Sartre. He talks about Sartre's racism (read anti-Semitism) and declares that such matters are meaningless. He places him above Michel Foucault seemingly because of Sartre's ability to ignore inconvenient facts. Lévy acknowledges that the Stalinism departs from Sartre's own principles, but it matters not. This is a man who even denounced Nikita Khrushchev's denunciation of Stalin. It is a picture of a man completely divorced from reality and his own work, and ultimately only in love with his own image. One thinks of a Soviet sycophant like Vladimir Posner who, after the fall, explained that he could only say the outrageous things he did to prevent his family from being sent to the gulag. One never understands Sartre's motive.

After more than 500 pages, the author can no more explain Sartre than anyone who has read Sartre's bibliography and then read one of his bilious interviews. This is not Lévy's failure, because he knows that he has attempted to explain a sphinx. It will be interesting to see if in 200 or 300 years the nightmare of the 20th century will be so distant that Sartre or Foucault or Bertrand Russell can be read in isolation. Right now I think they are best explained by Voltaire's statement "those who believe in absurdities will commit atrocities."

22 July 2006

on reading Santini

Joy in the Morning by P.G. Wodehouse

It was with some surprise that 20 pages into this book I realized that I had read it before, but under its original American title *Jeeves in the Morning*. It probably should not have been surprising, for the Wooster and Jeeves surface plots are all quite similar: avoidance of troubling older relatives and escaping betrothal. It is on the level of the subplot and the superb use of language that the books differ from one another.

If the essence of humor is the art of indirection, it is more Wodehouse's mastery of verbal indirection than the surprises of the plot that makes us laugh out loud. He was the master of the hypallage (also called a *transferred epithet* as when he writes at the beginning of *Jeeves and the Feudal Spirit* "as I sat in the bathtub soaping a meditative foot") as well as what can only be described as the "moronic pronouncement" of which Bertie, who is after all an Oxonian, is the master. It is all of this that makes Wodehouse not only irresistible, but in Bertie's words, makes one feel *boomps-a-daisy*.

But how does Wodehouse do this? His humor is as educated or perhaps more so than either Waugh or Powell, who both were graduates of Balliol College, Oxford, while Wodehouse's formal education ended at Dulwich College, a preparatory school on the edge of London. His biographer tells us many facts about him, but does not tell us much of anything that would cause us to believe that a clerk for the Hong Kong and Shanghai Bank would be reborn at an early age, almost Venus-like, as the master of learned wit, the creator of Psmith and Ukridge as well as Lord Emsworth and Uncle Fred (a.k.a the Earl of Ickenham) whose throwaway lines of literary learnedness could be the basis for a seminar in themselves. It is no less a mystery than the appearance of Shakespeare's genius, and there is no Earl of Oxford as a backup explanation.

There appear to be two questions that Wodehouse's definitive biographer (or any other that I am aware of) cannot answer. What did he read and when did he read it? Those are probably things that we cannot know about any great autodidact, Wodehouse being one, Faulkner another and, of course, Shakespeare. It is decidedly different with a writer like Yeats, whose progress is fairly easily tracked because of the massive output of reviews, essays, and polemics that parallel his verse and plays.

Never mind. It does not matter, for geniuses do spring full blown from the brow of Zeus.

In *Joy in the Morning*, Bertram finds himself trapped. While dropping into a bookstore (a place quite foreign to him) for the purpose of buying a copy of Spinoza as a reward for Jeeves, he bumps into Florence Craye, one of his many ex-fiancees. She mistakes the order he places for a sign that Bertie has become serious, and, as Bertie says, "It's extraordinary how one yields to that fatal temptation to swank." So we are naturally off to Florence's family seat at Steeple Bumpleigh and her tyrannical father, Lord Worplesdon. His Lordship happens now to be married to Bertie's even more frightening Aunt Agatha. Add to this Florence's current and very menacing fiance, Stilton Cheesewright, a former classmate of Bertie's, who has become a policeman, and the thwarted engagement of Bertie's friend Boko Fittleworth and Lord Worplesdon's ward Zenobia (Nobby) Hopwood, and you have the usual sublime Wodehouse mix.

Bertram tells the tale as a reflection on how all of this very nearly led him to despair, but now, riding back to London with Jeeves at the wheel, and because of Jeeves, all is once again boomps-a-daisy. And when we reflect on despair, it is so by the grace of Wodehouse.

Evelyn Waugh wrote that Wodehouse was an essentially indestructible writer who, in his words may release future generations from a captivity even more irksome than our own. This will only be true, I fear, until some aspect of his writing is deemed politically incorrect. It happened before, of course. He was nearly denied an OBE in his lifetime because the Labour Government then in power (Harold Wilson) thought he represented Britain's frivolous, bourgeois past.

22 May 2006

Understanding Anthony Powell by Nicholas Birns

I met Mr. Birns very briefly in December 2005 at the biennial conference of the Anthony Powell Society held at the Wallace Collection in London. The Wallace Collection is the home of Poussin's painting *A Dance to the Music of Time*, which inspired Powell's 12-volume cycle of novels by the same name, and thus was the most appropriate place to celebrate Mr. Powell's centenary. Mr. Birns teaches at the New School in New York, is an American, and is probably the youngest devotee of Mr. Powell to have written anything substantial about him.

This book is very much a "how to read," or a handbook if you will, and does not assume (as I do assume) that most of Anthony Powell's followers are believers in the magic of the "Brideshead Generation" (Powell, Waugh, Graham Greene, Harold Acton) and can therefore easily assimilate the milieu of prewar and immediate postwar Mayfair, Bloomsbury, and Belgravia as well as the bohemian and publishing worlds of London at those times.

The book is divided into roughly three parts: pre-Dance, the 12 volumes of Dance, and the post-Dance novels. It does not treat Powell's voluminous works of autobiography (gathered under the general title *To Keep the Ball Rolling*), diary, and criticism (much of which is gathered in a wonderful volume entitled *Miscellaneous Verdicts*). Given that Powell is now a cottage industry unto himself, and that Ms. Hilary Spurling has signed up to produce an authoritative biography, one assumes that these other works will receive their due.

Although this book presents a good discussion of *A Dance to the Music of Time*, I think Mr. Birns misses a point that many of my fellow Powell devotees miss. It is common among us to say that the narrator of the 12 volumes, Nicholas Jenkins, is not a confessional narrator and is more concerned with the spiderweb of connections of the various characters that appear and reappear. I think that this is only partially true.

Nick actually tells us a great deal about himself up to the time of his meeting of Lord Erridge's sister Lady Isobel and their subsequent marriage. It requires no special knowledge to see this coinciding directly with Powell's own marriage to Lady Violet. It is only after this that Powell shifts the focus entirely away from the narrator's personal life, which had previously included a fair amount of detail of his affair with Jean Duport, the married sister of his boyhood friend Peter Templer. After the marriage, the antihero, Kenneth Windmerpool, takes center stage. It is after this, probably naturally, that the coincidental "runnings into" become frequent: Windmerpool's disastrous marriage to Pamela Flitton, Nick's school friend Stringham's niece (her mother, Stringham's sister, has the best name in all of the books: Flavia Wisebite). Pamela may or may not be Flavia's daughter by the Errol Flynn-like cad, Dicky Umfraville.

What happens, I think, is that Lady Isobel is so clearly Lady Violet, more so even than the character X Trapnel being Julian McLaren-Ross, or Quiggin being Eric Blair/George Orwell, that Powell gave up revealing anything of himself or his family.

In discussing what ought to be a critic's overriding concern, that of the coincidences that drive the narrative, Birns is rather perfunctory. I think Evelyn Waugh on this subject, in his unfinished autobiography *A Little Learning*, is more apposite:

In reading his brilliant series of novels I have sometimes thought—and, indeed, have been so foolish as to state as much in a review—that the recurring seemingly haphazard conjunctions of human life, which comprise his theme, pass beyond plausibility. His hero's passage through youth and early manhood is continually recrossed in improbable circumstances by the same characters. After I had written the review expressing doubts on the authenticity of so many coincidences, I began to reflect on my own acquaintance with him and understood that his was genuine social realism. At Oxford we stood on friendly terms though barely in friendship. We have seldom met by arrangement and often there have been long periods when we never met at all. But this is a chart of our courses. Three years after going down, as I shall relate, I tried to learn cabinet making at the L.C.C. school in Southampton Row. There in the same drawing class I found Tony, who was studying typography. A little later, very hard up and seeking a commission to write a book, it was Tony who introduced me to my first publisher. When he married, it was to the sister of the girl with whom my first wife shared lodgings. During the latter part of the war he worked in the same department of the War Office as my brother-in-law and shared a house with him in Regent's Park. When he settled in the country he chose a house within a mile or two of Mells, with which I had formed close links. I suppose in the looser society of the United States or in the tighter society of, say, France such fortuitous connections would be barely possible. It is one of Tony's achievements to record this interplay which, I think is essentially English.

This says in a paragraph what Birns labors through an entire book (an enjoyable one) to say. It also lays out something that I think is not quite true. If one charts the course of educated white Southerners in the 20th century, I would guess (just based on my own experience) that you would find the same crisscrossing pattern. I should like very much someday to write an essay on that very subject.

The thing Birns does not address at all, nor have I seen it addressed anywhere in the vast arcana of Powell studies, is the meaning of the three naked women: when Jean Duport meets

Nick at the door of her flat in just carpet slippers, the maid in a flashback to Nick's childhood at dinner during a visit by General Conyers, and Pamela Flitton when she is carrying on with the American Gwinnett who is studying X Trapnel. Perhaps that will be my next undertaking, but I shall not try to tie it to anything historical, for Mr. Powell would wink at us and say, "that is not the way fiction is written."

1 July 2006

The Living Thoughts of Kierkegaard By W.H. Auden

As best I can recall, the definition of existentialism involves something about the displacement of the individual in the modern world and (at least in Kierkegaard's case) the resultant leap to faith. W.H Auden compiled short portions of Kierkegaard's work-some epigrammatic, some more discursive—more than half a century ago as he was making his own journey from leftist orthodoxy to Christian apologist in the rubble of the post–World War II world.

To read this after having read Bernard-Henri Lévy's volume on Sartre is to recognize what an elastic term existentialism is, or has become, to the point that most uses of the word are nearly meaningless, having come to represent anything outside ourselves that we do not understand. It is also quite impossible, I think, for those of us who have lived in a world where the theories of Freud have always existed to comprehend that in Kierkegaard's time, agonizing introspection was much the exception rather than the norm. Further, introspection based on a set of generally poorly understood concepts (such as Freud or Jung) was nonexistent.

It is also good to remember that Auden edited this book in the gloom of the immediate postwar world when he, and many others, believed that the bourgeois society that had emerged in the early 19th century was now dead, at least in Europe, with perhaps the United States soon to follow. This was something that was believed to one degree or another by both left and right, believer and nonbeliever, from Sartre on one side to James Burnham on the other. It is clear that in his selections here, Auden is trying to create, for his own sake, something approaching hope.

Kierkegaard is not a systematic philosopher and in fact states an unqualified suspicion of systematic philosophy. Within his own circumscribed system, this makes sense. From the viewpoint of Kierkegaard, the journey ends with the leap to faith—or as he puts it, without risk there can be no faith, which seems rather the opposite formulation of Pascal's wager. The corollary to this, it seems to me, is that any attempt at a unified system of philosophy would be to deny the basis for faith. In that respect, it is not unlike Gödel's incompleteness theorem, which in one of its aspects holds that the only mind that could comprehend a complete set would be the mind of God, which can hold all things at once. We cannot know God's mind, and therefore we must accept or, if you will, believe.

What is more apparent here, and what is consistent with what I perceive to be Auden's mindset at the close of World War II, is Kierkegaard's despair over the changed world in which he finds himself. In this respect he is very much like Nietzsche. Both have a mistrust of democracy and both make a leap, Kierkegaard to faith, Nietzsche to something more ambiguous. In the preface, Auden selected an aphorism that sums this up:

Fundamentally Hegel makes men into heathens, into a race of animals gifted with reason. For in the animal world "the individual" is always less important than the race. But it is the peculiarity of the human race that just because the individual is created in the image of God, "the individual" is above the race.

—from Prefatory Aphorisms (italics mine)

One is tempted to think of the writings of Eric Hoffer, particularly *The Ordeal of Change,* and how men make bad choices out of their fundamental fear of that dreaded thing. It is this fundamental fear that leads to totalitarian states. Without knowing it, I think, Hannah Arendt and Karl Popper begin from the same premise. They, while not adopting the political or economic philosophy of a von Hayek or von Mises, recognize that the solution to the chaos of bourgeois society is an inner strength, not an all-controlling government. Kierkegaard's answer to chaos is also that type of inner strength, but the kind brought on by faith. If one measures Kierkegaard by Jean-François Revel's dictum that philosophers need to ask the question "how should men live," he comes closer than most.

17 July 2006

Thomas

The Breaking Point: Hemingway, Dos Passos, and the Murder of Jose Robles by Stephen Koch

I read somewhere that upon first meeting in the 1920s, Ezra Pound said that he admired Ernest Hemingway for his directness in his prose, but also for his "American tough-guy" persona. This book, which is an important contribution to understanding the Lost Generation and the writers that followed, suffers from its poor imitation of that tough-guy style. It also suffers from the substitution of a stream-of-consciousness set of endnotes in lieu of a formal bibliography and index. That is a shame, because this is an important work about Hemingway's short flirtation with the international Left.

Looking back at the two most notable Hemingway biographies, Carlos Baker's *Ernest Hemingway: A Life Story* and Jeffrey Meyers's multivolume study, we see that Hemingway's rift with John Dos Passos during the Spanish Civil War is treated only in passing, and the murder of Dos Passos's friend Jose Robles is a bare notation. Meyers described a confrontation between Hemingway and Dos Passos at Gerald and Sara Murphy's New York apartment after their time in Spain, but both books leave a great deal of mystery, perhaps hoping to leave Hemingway some dignity in what appears to have been a low point in his mistreatment of friends and general self-indulgence. It is something neither the Murphys nor Dos Passos ever record, despite the deplorable treatment they later received at Hemingway's hands in *A Moveable Feast*. Koch's version of the incident shows it to be consistent with Hemingway's ego-driven bad behavior throughout the time of the Spanish Civil War.

At least two of the reviews I have read of this book have

focused on Hemingway's self-destructive tendencies. In one stroke he destroys his marriage to his second wife, Pauline, by taking Martha Gellhorn (ultimately his third wife) to Spain with him and at the same time destroys his friendship with Dos Passos. I think this book tells us about more than just the nature of Hemingway's need to destroy; it demonstrates how Hemingway's insatiable ego allowed him to become, at least for a time, a dupe of the Popular Front and ultimately the Soviets.

If this book were equipped with a suitable index and bibliography rather than lengthy endnotes that serve almost as a second narrative, it would be easier to tell how much of the story of Jose Robles was already known and how much comes from the author's original research in the Hemingway, Dos Passos, and other archives (most notably that of the leftist writer Josephine Herbst, who was present for much of what transpires in the book).

Carlos Baker, in his three-paragraph treatment of the Robles matter, attributes Hemingway's behavior to his pride at being part of the in crowd in Madrid. Koch goes much further and shows Hemingway's manipulation by the Soviets. Here he relies not only on the Herbst archives but also on the 1990 revision of Robert Conquest's *The Great Terror*, which benefited from the opening of archives in Moscow and laid out much more about Soviet involvement in Spain than was generally known when Baker wrote his book in the late 1960s. Conquest makes clear that Stalin never had any intention of giving the Loyalists enough help to win. His real efforts were directed at achieving the 1939 nonaggression pact with Hitler's Germany and continuing to destroy his internal enemies (real or imagined).

Koch also relies on Amanda Vaill's splendid book about Gerald and Sara Murphy, *Everybody Was So Young*. Vaill is particularly good about Hemingway's incomparable ability to seek revenge on anyone who had been kind to him.

Although the reviewers are correct in picking up on the fact that Hemingway had an almost pathological need to damage those around him, the question they seem to ignore, which I think Koch tries very hard to answer, is how Hemingway was so duped when Dos Passos, who began the Spanish Civil War as a committed leftist, was not. Hemingway wrote the propaganda play *The Fifth Column*; he took over Dos Passos's original project, which became the documentary film *The Spanish Earth* and was celebrated by André Malraux in France and by the *Daily Worker* in the United States. Yet, by the time Hemingway published his main work to come out of the War, *For Whom the Bell Tolls*, its hero Robert Jordan is made to say things that clearly convince the reader that he believes nothing the Russian advisers tell him.

Hemingway is often thought, at least in part, to have killed himself because he could not write anymore. One can trace his decline to the Spanish Civil War in much the same way one can trace Truman Capote's long crash landing to the publication of *In Cold Blood*. In both cases, the writer became more celebrity than writer and denied himself the ability to seal himself away and sift the facts. When that happened, he was finished.

9 July 2006

Note: Since then, I have watched again the movie *For Whom the Bell Tolls*. Perhaps there is more balance there because of the script-writers. Or perhaps it is because for Hemingway to get it right, he simply had to destroy those he loved, Martha Gellhorn and John Dos Passos, both left and right.

29 August 2006

A Writer's Life by Gay Talese

The reviewers have essentially called this a mess of a book. It is that; it is also one I love to distraction. This probably has more to do with the fact that I remain fascinated by the now old story of the New Journalism. Anything about Tom Wolfe, Jimmy Breslin, or even Norman Mailer; the founding of *New York Magazine*; and the heyday of *Esquire* in the late 1960s fascinates me.

The reviewers have focused on the fact that this is a book about being unable to write a book. I think the disappointment comes from the fact that, despite the title, it is really not an autobiography but a pastiche of several failed ideas for books. Among these are the history of a series of failed restaurants in the same building on East 63rd Street in Manhattan, the John and Lorena Bobbit penis-severing saga, and the fate of the female Chinese soccer player who blew the last play in the finals held in the Rose Bowl in 1999. Interspersed in the narrative are glimpses, but only just that, of the author's life.

Talese is not a confessional author, but when one thinks of the New Journalists, only Mailer is of the self-absorbed, navel-gazing variety that can make the rather dreary life of a writer a best seller. Talese can tell you clearly what seems to be going on in Frank Sinatra's mind, as he did in the famous piece "Frank Sinatra Has a Cold," but he is not about to tell you much about himself. He tells us that after an initial spat with his in-laws after he got married, he never saw them again. I am just interested enough in the salacious to want to know why, but he closes the door as soon as he opens it.

What he does tell us is that he is incapable of writing the kind of short volume that is really an extended essay, such as Tom Wolfe did in both *The Painted Word* and *From Bauhaus to Our House*.

Each of the short pieces that make up this book could have been something like that and given him four books over a 10-year period instead of one book about not being able to write a book. Let me modify that. Above and beyond the initial topic, the Bobbits are deeply uninteresting people. Which is what Tina Brown, then editor of *The New Yorker*, told Talese when he was researching it for the magazine.

The extent to which Talese keeps himself out of the story makes it difficult for us to feel the anguish he clearly wants to tell us about. One can imagine someone like the outsized novelist Pat Conroy putting his anguish before the reader like wringing out a towel. I mention him because Conroy's editor is, of course, Nan Talese.

Nevertheless, Gay Talese writes with a precision and clarity that make him a delight to read, a style that dazzles you simply because it is not trying to dazzle you. He is the legitimate successor to the Harold Ross, William Shawn, and E.B. White school of concision. When he does finally digress to tell you something personal, about his student days at Alabama or the history of his marriage, we are interested and we wish he would tell us more. Perhaps that is the difference between a natural reporter and a natural storyteller. Perhaps he needs to have more than E.B. White's single martini to gain the courage he needs to get started.

23 July 2006

Somerset Maugham: A Life by Jeffrey Meyers

Among the more curious volumes in my highly eclectic and perhaps simply odd library is a copy of W. Somerset Maugham's version of autobiography, *The Summing Up*, inscribed by the author to the actress Mary Astor. This would have been not long after her turn as Brigid O'Shaughnessy opposite Humphrey Bogart's Sam Spade in John Huston's *The Maltese Falcon*. The fact that a movie star had such a volume reminds us first, that Maugham was really the first superstar novelist of the 20th century (well before Hemingway), and second, that up until 40 or so years ago, popular fiction was more accomplished and perhaps more serious than it is today.

Jeffrey Meyers, whose ability to churn out what seems like a book a year (and whose only challenger in that regard is the prolific Garry Wills) has written about Scott Fitzgerald, Hemingway in a thorough multivolume study, and assorted other topics. Nevertheless, Maugham seems an odd choice, not because Maugham's was not an interesting life but because his work has been out of fashion for so long. Whereas Meyers can write volumes about Hemingway, knowing he will at least provoke a debate in the academy and in the pages of serious journals, Maugham, I would think, only raises a yawn, being regarded as wholly conventional in his approach to telling a story, basely commercial, and, worst of all in this confessional world, ill at ease with his own homosexuality. This despite the fact that within the last decade two movies have been made from Maugham stories: the execrable remake of *The Razor's Edge* and the rather delightful adaptation of the book *Theatre* into the movie *Being Julia*.

The loneliness and desolation of Maugham's upbringing recur throughout his work, most notably in *Of Human Bondage*, published in 1915. This reminds us that Maugham overlapped Henry James and Joseph Conrad for nearly a generation.

Meyers reinforces the image we have of Maugham as the ultimate middlebrow writer. I am not certain that this is necessarily the way to view him. Another perspective is that he was continuing the straight narrative tradition of Thackery and Dickens stretching back to Henry Fielding at a time when Conrad began to experiment with interior monologue, Joyce moved on to true stream of consciousness, and Hemingway, as Pound liked to think of him, dealt with directness and immediacy.

This is much the same as Sergei Rachmaninoff writing his lush and almost perfect Second Symphony, the epitome of the Romantic spirit, while Stravinsky and Schoenberg were experimenting with radically different forms of music that were nonmelodic (which can be likened to the absence of plot in narrative fiction) leading to atonal music or music on a 12-tone system.

Of Maugham's personal life we are told everything, or what seems like nearly everything, considering that Maugham was a mostly closeted homosexual who destroyed most of his correspondence. He was married and had a daughter and had two long-term relationships: first with American Gerald Haxton and, after Haxton died in the midst of the Second World War, with the Englishman Alan Searle. Maugham suffered from a stammer, was short and unattractive, and was bullied at school. Instead of going to university he became a medical doctor and was well acquainted with the human detritus that were the London slums at the end of the 19th century, thus, the pictures of the underside that dominate *Liza of Lambeth* and *Of Human Bondage.*

His range of subjects and his range of abilities as a writer were astonishing. He was at once the most popular novelist in England and in many ways its most popular playwright, the best writer of short stories since Guy de Maupassant, an essayist, and a critic. He began collecting art after his first literary successes at the turn of the century, and when he disposed of the Picassos, Cézannes, and Gauguins in the 1950s, they were as the collection of a plutocrat like Norton Simon or J. Paul Getty, yet he had bought them early on for practically nothing. One of his last books, *Purely For My Pleasure*, shows off his art collection.

Because Maugham was an astute businessman and ended up wealthy, we are to believe that he was a second-rate writer. Meyers does nothing to contradict this perception. There is no cause and effect. Shakespeare was a first-rate businessman, whose acumen allowed him to retire in comfort to Stratford-on-Avon. W.B. Yeats, on the cutting edge of modernism, managed to live quite comfortably. If something in Maugham's work leaves him at a deficit, it was not because he was a success in managing the business side of his career. Rather, I think, it was the absence of the spark or the muse that moves a supertalented writer.

It seems at heart, Maugham believed in nothing and looked for nothing to believe in, despite the nods in that direction contained in *The Razor's Edge*. He was, in fact, a lifelong homosexual, ambivalent about his situation, who maintained a marriage to a woman he loathed for many years. He was a liberal, a supporter of the Labour Party's agenda, who lived a large part of his life as a tax exile in the south of France. He was, at his center from all appearances, a mostly unhappy person.

None of this means much. That he did not arise to the performance of a writer like Yeats or Proust is beside the point. He provided entertainment of a very high quality to the reading and theater-going public for nearly 70 years. That a book like *Theatre* can still entertain us as the movie *Being Julia* explains more about him than an analysis of the failure of his work against a modernist yardstick. He was first and foremost a Victorian-cum-Edwardian, and they do not digress to tell all.

10 August 2006

The Great Terror: A Reassessment by Robert Conquest

Of the many things I wish I could have attended, but was of the wrong generation, were the "fascist lunches" of Kingsley Amis and Robert Conquest, also known as the Kingers and Conquers lunches. I read about them a year or so ago in Martin Amis's book *Koba the Dread*, a book in which Amis contemplated how his father could have swallowed the Stalinist line up until the Hungarian uprising of 1956. His incredulity at his father's beliefs and those of his own best friend, Christopher Hitchens, who came unmoored from the Soviets somewhat later, was sparked by Conquest's massive documentation of what was known contemporaneously about Stalin's terror. This, added to Orwell's writing about the Popular Front in *Homage to Catalonia*, helps one draw the conclusion that ignorance of Stalin's murder of 20 million of his own people could be due only to willful ignorance.

Conquest's book, a massive revision of the 1970 original, was published in 1990 and based on archives opened for the first time in the early days of Glasnost. The detail of torture; shootings; rape of the daughters of the accused in their presence; and the NKVD, the leading secret police organization, sending the children of Stalin's victims to orphanages is truly mind numbing. More baffling still was Stalin's ability to shuffle in one group of lackeys to rat on one another and then smoothly replace them with another group. Yagoda gave way to Yezhov as head of the NKVD, who then gave way to perhaps the most demented butcher of them all, Lavrenti Beria.

What this expanded and brutal recounting, almost day by day, of the slaughter accomplishes is to put the lie to something I heard many people from my earliest childhood say. The statement always went like this, "Well, no matter how bad things are under (you name it, Stalin, Castro, Mao), the people are better off than they were under (the Tsar, Batista, Emperor of China). Conquest's quote from Camus is exactly on point: "None of the evils which totalitarianism . . . claims to remedy is worse than totalitarianism itself."

Conquest gives us a precise history of the Russian Revolution and of Bolshevik rule up to the undermining of Zinoviev and Bukharin by Stalin just before and contemporaneous with Lenin's death. He brings into perspective the idea that Russia, consisting mostly of peasants, was the last place that Marx would have picked for a proletarian revolution because, for one thing, it did not have much of a proletariat. Lenin believed he could create a worker's state only after he had created a sufficient industrial state to begin with, thus the digression in the 1920s of the New Economic Policy.

What one gleans here and in Amis's book *Koba the Dread*, and in his autobiography, *Experience*, is that Stalin only had the crudest understanding of Marxist–Leninist theory, and that it is wrong to attribute to him a motive like Mao's—a mad desire to implement his theories in their purest form. In the end, the slaughter and destruction are the same, but Stalin's sole motive from beginning to end was absolute power.

One wonders if in looking at the big three butchers of the 20th century there are degrees when it comes to being despicable. One wonders also what it was that Stalin aspired to be. Hitler aspired to be an artist, and Germany was his canvas: the Nuremberg rallies, the Leni Riefenstahl movies. Mao sought nothing less than to tear civilization away from the mooring of several thousand years, and the carnage is proof that an intellectual in power is almost by definition a dangerous crackpot. Who did Stalin want to be? Perhaps it was Napoleon—to be absolute master of a state he built himself. Yet, unlike Napoleon, who forced the implementation of reforms that work to this day, no one seems to have much information on what Stalin thought about. His intelligence always seems to be of the type that belongs to a petty criminal. Like Napoleon, he was only a peripheral player in the revolution that brought his faction to power, but unlike Napoleon, was not recognized for his brilliance by most of those around him. We cannot imagine Marshall Ney meeting Stalin on return from exile on Elba and suddenly changing sides. Stalin took no gambles. He ruled strictly from his sense of paranoia. And from abilities that could be attributed to an idiot savant, he played one leader off against another, one faction off against another until no one was left standing. Conquest tells us that the great purges came more or less to an end in 1938 because the requirement that those arrested denounce other "enemies of the state" was rapidly leading to the unmanageable result that most of the population would be in jail awaiting liquidation.

Conquest, writing in 1990 and applauding the opening of archives that give such gruesome detail, says that the Russian people were at last headed for freedom, but warned there could be relapses along the way. It must be the present moment of Putin's state oligarchs that he envisioned, but the world knows about this. What has emerged is the inability to return the genie of information to the bottle. Putin may control newspapers and television the way Stalin did, but the information age has deprived the West the ability to ever say again, "We did not know."

15 August 2006

Empire: A Novel by Gore Vidal

I have now read four of Gore Vidal's books that have the subtitle "A Novel." I have read them in order of the events they chronicle and not the order in which they were written. The entire saga covers the beginning of the republic with *Burr* and ends with (I believe, not having read it) *Washington, D.C.*, chronicling the rise of JFK. Vidal's none-too-subtle theory is that, beginning with Lincoln's invocation of the implied powers of the office of President, urged upon him by his Secretary of State William Seward, the United States ceased to be a republic, and like Rome (in the words of the poet Robinson Jeffers) slowly descended into empire.

Like all of the works in the series that I have read, Vidal's own massive condescension comes through in the narrative, although in this particular volume I think he does this through the very real personage of Henry Adams, whose prose style Vidal seems to consciously imitate. But even through that guise, one hears the unmistakable voice of Vidal saying, "Oh, don't you tell me. I know better than you."

For those of us coming of age in the 1960s, Gore Vidal was one of the combatants refereed by Howard K. Smith at the 1968 Democratic and Republican political conventions. It was during one such engagement (I believe during the Democratic convention) that Vidal called his opponent William Buckley a crypto-Nazi, to which Buckley responded by saying, "Listen you queer, call me a Nazi again, and I'll sock you in your god damned mouth." It may have been that very moment that gave birth to the political shout shows like *Crossfire* and *The O'Reilly Factor*. I'd like to think not, in view of the 30-plus years of civilized discourse Buckley had on *Firing Line*.

That said, Vidal's career has been one of marked literary

accomplishment, running parallel to the careers of his two great hates (who were and are almost exactly the same age and in many ways equally or more accomplished): Truman Capote and Buckley himself (he had to give up hating Bobby Kennedy after he died). He has moved between life as an expatriate in Italy to occasional forays into American politics, such as his run for the U.S. Senate in California. He also had a bizarre correspondence with Timothy McVeigh, the Oklahoma City Bomber, just prior to the latter's execution, that was published in *Vanity Fair.*

This volume continues the story of Charlie Schuyler's family. Schuyler was the purported author of half of *Burr* (the other half being from suppositious Revolutionary War diaries of Burr). He was also (along with Martin van Buren) thought by many in that and the succeeding volumes to be the illegitimate son of Aaron Burr. Here we focus on Caroline Sanford, Charlie's granddaughter, who has been raised in France but comes to America after her father's death. With two half brothers, her family lineage seems reminiscent of the Vidal–Auchincloss–Bouvier arrangement.

Caroline's half-brother Blaise is a Yale man, a friend of Del Hay, the son of Secretary of State John Hay, from whose point of view much of *Lincoln* was written, and aide-de-camp to William Randolph Hearst. William McKinley is in the White House and the United States has just concluded that "splendid little war" with Spain, acquiring Puerto Rico and the Philippines together with hegemony over Cuba in the process.

Caroline, single minded, the disguised European sophisticate viewing American innocence firsthand, is a most Jamesian character. She buys a failing newspaper in Washington, D.C., partly because she wants to, but mostly to thwart Hearst who wants the paper. At this point I was poised for the emergence of a prototype for Katharine Graham set in an earlier era. That is not what happened. Vidal is more interested in giving us an imagined first-hand version of what occurred in the administrations of William McKinley and Theodore Roosevelt.

McKinley he treats with only a modest amount of the trademark disdain, portraying him as an honest and thoughtful man. This is much the way he also seems to see Dwight Eisenhower in retrospect, based on what he said about him in an interview with Dick Cavett a number of years ago and what he has written in his first volume of autobiography, *Palimpsest*.

TR, on the other hand (to use the word E.B. White used in his obituary of *The New Yorker's* founding editor, Harold Ross), always obtrudes. TR is a combination of grand egoist and political hypocrite. By contrast, the other great mover of the book, William Randolph Hearst, comes off as a megalomaniac and a scoundrel, but much the way Lyndon Johnson is rendered by Robert Caro, as a larger-than-life character who is infinitely interesting.

After getting through all of this, including a graphic sex scene that is so mechanical as to leave one depressed rather than aroused, one is left to wonder what it is Vidal wants us to think. He wants us to believe we have given up the republic of the founders for an empire. He comes across as a snob (albeit an entertaining one) who manages at once to believe himself an aristocrat-intellectual and otherwise—and a believer in populism.

Where he misses the boat is in focusing on forms of government more than on thinking in terms of the origin and nature of freedom. Freedom is not given to us by the framers of our government or the enactor of our laws. It is the thing we choose to yield, voluntarily or sometimes involuntarily perhaps for the common good or the common peace, to government.

He leaves a foretaste of things to come, having Hearst tell

us he would stick it to the British by sending an Irish-American as ambassador to the Court of St. James. I cannot wait to see how he treats the fictional Joseph P. Kennedy (with whom Franklin Roosevelt did just that) versus the way he has treated the real one.

One marvels nonetheless at the research that has gone into these books. And I suppose they come as close to entertainment as anything I read. Vidal is a workmanlike writer. Unlike his nemesis Truman Capote, he cannot make language soar. But then again, *In Cold Blood* to the side, Capote was essentially a polisher and a miniaturist. Vidal's feelings toward Capote are revealed in this flippant comment to Johnny Carson when Capote died at Carson's ex-wife's house, "Don't feel bad Johnny, I promise to die at your house."

14 September 2006

The Man From New York: John Quinn and His Friends
by B.L. Reid

This book won the Pulitzer Prize for biography in 1969. I remember checking it out of the Rialto, California, public library at the time, glancing at it because I was interested in the photographic illustrations, many of them contemporary with the pictures in Hemingway's *A Moveable Feast* and then returning it to the library mostly unread.

It is well to remember in reading it now two things: First, it was at the very beginning of the era of the monster, no-detail-lost biography that persists to this day. The second is that the variety of topics that encompassed Quinn's life (the Irish literary and dramatic movements, modernism in both literature and art, Irish independence, New York Democratic party politics) has been the subject of an immense amount of scholarship since that time.

The ensuing 37 years have seen the publication of Michael Holroyd's four-volume biography of Shaw, Richard Ellmann's comprehensive biography of Oscar Wilde, Roy Foster's two-volume biography of Yeats, several sizable books on Pound, as well as Richardson's two volumes on Picasso, and Hilary Spurling's two volumes on Matisse. And all of these subjects intersected the relatively brief life of John Quinn, who died in 1922 at the age of 54, just as modernism came into its own.

The bare outline of Quinn's life is impressive enough—a wealthy successful lawyer at a young age, although he came from a modest Midwestern background. Yet hardly had his professional career taken off when his days became filled with the efforts of the arts, first championing the Irish renaissance, W.B. Yeats, Lady Gregory, Jack Butler Yeats, and, as patron in New York for the odd manuscript of *Ulysses*.

When he found out he was dying, he ordered his will in such a way as to sell off everything, with the money going to his sisters and their children (he never married) with no thought of keeping his incomparable collection together. It would be another four years before the founding of the Museum of Modern Art of New York, which would have been jump-started by his collection. The only bequest in his will to an institution was Georges Seurat's *Le Cirque* to the Louvre.

One is left then with the memory of a man who collected, as Somerset Maugham put it, purely for his pleasure. And what a pleasure it must have been.

24 October 2006

The Unknown Matisse: A Life of Henri Matisse: The Early Years, 1869-1908 by Hilary Spurling

One of the difficulties in reading the biography of a visual artist such as Matisse, at least for me, is a fundamental ignorance of the materials and techniques that go into such an artist's work. Above and beyond the obvious, such as the fundamental change brought on by the first impressionists, or the even starker change wrought by Picasso and Braque with the advent of cubism, it is more difficult for me to understand the evolution of a painter than it is, say, of a composer whose materials I understand to some extent and whose evolution I can therefore more readily comprehend.

At the same time, when the artist is a very public figure, like Pablo Picasso, whose life is the stuff of myth, it is easy to be distracted from the art and artist by the man. This is why I found James Lord's *Picasso and Dora* so fascinating, and, although Lord doubtless has a profound understanding of Picasso's work, his memoir did not really do anything to increase mine, and perhaps it was not meant to. I have yet to struggle through Lord's competitor for Picasso's attention, John Richardson's two-volume definitive biography, and that may be where what I seek is to be found.

Henri Matisse, on the other hand, seems (at least within the bohemian art world he inhabited) to have worked hard and then otherwise led the life of a good burgher. It is true that early on he fathered a daughter out of wedlock, but he was able to raise that daughter happily with the two sons from his marriage, the daughter becoming closer to her stepmother than to her biological mother. It is also well to remember that in France up to the beginning of the 20th century, illegitimacy was common anywhere below the upper bourgeoisie, primarily because of the taxes required to enact a marriage ceremony. At least that is what I remember from some of Émile Zola's deeply depressing works.

The premise that Miss Spurling tries to set up is that there was a moment when Matisse changed from simply the academically trained evolving postimpressionist painter to a genius who was able to take the elements of form and color and by separating them, do something absolutely revolutionary with them. I am skeptical of such alleged moments of sudden afflatus, such as the belief that Yeats suddenly became a modern poet only after being mesmerized by Ezra Pound in the summer of 1913.

Closer to the heart of what happens, I think, is that in any endeavor, but especially in the visual and musical arts, when the prevailing standard becomes so wrapped up in its own set of techniques, a movement to simplify can always assume the artistic high ground. One can almost characterize this as the rococo effect. All movements, whether it is French academic painting or German baroque music, reach a point where most of what needs to be said has been said and the movement itself becomes effete and worn out. At a very simple level one can look at American popular music over the course of the 20th century, which started from New Orleans and Chicago jazz in the early days, followed through the swing era, and then reached a stage after World War II at which the big band had become pretty much moribund. About the same time, real jazz soared off into its rococo, chamber music phase of bebop and what came after, and suddenly rock and roll took the stage with what was a more or less hillbilly simplicity.

What the author conveys here is that movement toward simplicity was born at an exhibition at the Independent's Salon in 1905 and more or less loosed modernism on the Parisian art world the way that the 1913 Armory Show did to America eight years later. This was the beginning of Fauvism, the beginning of line and color meaning more than actual representation. However, it did not convert everyone: Bernard Berenson never became a believer. From Miss Spurling's description, the grand revolution was, however, much more tied to academic discipline than one might suppose. It is certainly less tied to some overarching theory than abstract expressionism would be two generations later (at least according to Mr. Tom Wolfe) when the theory trumped the end result and certainly trumped the idea of pleasing the customer.

The question left unanswered in this book (which ends in 1908) is how much of Matisse's evolution is the departure of a genius and how much is simply a natural consequence of the flow that began with Cézanne. Again, the problem is doubtless more me than the author; the fact that I possess so little knowledge of the painter's tools. The avant-garde of the musical world at that time, such as Stravinsky, Schoenberg, and Alban Berg, worked with the same tool kit as their predecessors, so it is easier for me to understand how they used these to depart from the known way. I think of Waugh's sentence in *Brideshead Revisited* when Charles Ryder talks about feeling the brush come alive in his hand—and I wish that I knew enough to understand when that thrill possessed Matisse.

13 November 2006

Jean de Florette and Manon of the Springs
by Marcel Pagnol

My first recollection of seeing the name Marcel Pagnol was in the reviews of the movies made by Claude Berri of the two novels that collectively form the narrative *The Water of the Hills*. The two reviews I read (and reread every week in synopsis) were by Pauline Kael in *The New Yorker*. I recall her talking about Manon "settling his [Cesar Soubeyran's] hash" and referring to Cesar's nephew, Ugolin, as "cretinous." Those two characters were played by Yve Montand and Daniel Auteuil, respectively.

It had not originally been in my plan to read these books this year, they are not on the list. I read them as background for a trip we planned in the autumn to Provence. I read about half of *Jean de Florette* on the flight from Houston to Paris, finished it late one night in Fontvieille and read portions of *Manon* in Aix-en-Provence and then back in Paris and finished it the following week in Houston. After finishing them, I realized they were more than entertainment and background and made me think about why the French are so fond of Faulkner (I will not think about why they are so fond of Jerry Lewis).

Beyond the two Claude Berri movies, if Marcel Pagnol is known in this country at all it is for the English language movie version of one of the plays of his trilogy about Marseilles, *Fanny*. The movie starred Maurice Chevalier, Charles Boyer, and Leslie Caron. I chiefly remember it (to the extent I do remember, for the last time I saw it was on a black and white television, late at night in the late 1960s) for its lush score and my disappointment that Chevalier and Boyer were not playing upper-class swells but water-front proletariat.

It is well to remember that when Faulkner won the Nobel Prize in 1950, his work was essentially out of print in the United States. Where it was being read, by the likes of Sartre and Camus among others, was in France. The publication of these two volumes coincides with the publication of *The Town* and *The Mansion*. The Papet is a fair approximation of the itchy-palmed Flem Snopes (to borrow Walker Percy's description), and Ugolin could well stand in for any number of nitwit lesser Snopes.

We find also the erudite detachment of Faulkner's Gavin Stevens in the schoolmaster, who at the end marries the beautiful Manon. The schoolmaster is the same kind of pivot point as Gavin Stevens because he is above the clannishness of his birthplace and sees both the tragedy and the irony. The schoolmaster is, however, closer to prince charming than Gavin Stevens, who did, after all, cuckold the impotent Flem Snopes.

The difference between the two writers is that at the end, they give us an entirely different view of the same sometimes fine, sometimes degenerate world. Faulkner, for all the wisdom, ersatz and real, that is sometimes spouted in his works, is at base a cynic and terribly pessimistic. Pagnol, on the other hand, is very much a sentimentalist. Pagnol was a playwright and scenarist who sought to entertain. Faulkner wrote screenplays to make ends meet and at the end of the day was less interested in entertaining his audience than he was in informing them of his own dark vision of mankind. When Eula Varner commits suicide at the end of *The Town*, one can almost hear Beckett and Camus applauding in the background.

As befits him, Pagnol's story resolves itself with grace, courage, and hope. It even turns out that Cesar is Jean de Florette's natural father. The happy ending eluded Faulkner until he wrote *The Reivers*, but then again, in Mississippi you drink corn liquor, not pastis.

Marcel Pagnol is not, insofar as I am able to judge, a contemporary of the first French Existentialists in any way except time of birth. He seems more a successor to Edmond Rostard, of *Cyrano* and *The Romancers* (which, after all, became *The Fantisticks*.

9 October 2006

The Tin Drum by Günter Grass

In recent weeks, Günter Grass has published in German a memoir titled *Beim Haütem den Zwiebel* (Peeling the Onion) in which he reveals for the first time that during the Second World War he was a member of the Waffen S.S. Until now, my vague awareness of Grass had centered on his prominence as a reflexively anti-American European intellectual who seemed to be unquestioning in his championing of left-wing causes. Now there are calls for him to return his Nobel Prize and especially his freedom of the City of Gdansk. Gdansk, of course as the Free City of Danzig, is his birthplace and the setting of this, his first and most famous novel.

But what is this book? Is it an allegory of German history or perhaps a cynical form of magical realism? It is the memoir of the thoroughly addled Oskar Matzerath, written from a mental hospital. Oskar, who is able to recall and narrate a description of his own birth in 1921, decides at the age of three that he will stop growing. He remains such until he is 21, able only to play his tin drum and to break glass with a piercing scream.

The story follows the rise of the Nazis (whose initial rallies in the 1930s, Oskar interrupts with his scream, which can cut glass). Danzig was at the time a "free city" under the League of Nations, thus the slightly less sinister pall hanging over it until 1938 when Germany simply abrogated the League's mandate and began to use Danzig as a basis for confrontation with Poles. Living through the war and its aftermath, Oskar's adventures read like a dada nihilist version of *Candide*.

Oskar is neither as amusingly addled as the narrator of Nabokov's *Pale Fire*, nor is the terror of the war as immediate and crushing as in Jerzy Kosinski's *The Painted Bird*, which were published in 1961 and 1965, respectively, making them subsequent to the German publication of this work. One suspects that Nabo-kov still wins the contest of inventing the earliest and most aber-rant narrator in the form of Humbert Humbert in *Lolita*.

Throughout the narrative, Oskar speaks of himself in both the first and third person, often within the same paragraph and sometimes within the same sentence. Between this conceit and the episodic, almost picaresque, journey, the model of *Candide* comes even more alive. But Candide is making fun of theorists in general and Rousseau in particular. There is nothing mean spirited about it. What is little Oskar kidding us about?

Oskar talks to us from the insane asylum where he is being held. It is only at the very end of the story that we learn he is being held for the murder of Sister Dorothea, the nurse living in the same flat with him (among several rented rooms), whom he did not in fact kill.

Although he is held for a murder he did not commit, he believes that he and his drum are responsible for the deaths of his mother, her cousin Jan Bronski (who may or may not be his father), and his nominal father Matzerath. Is Günter Grass's point that Germany is punished only for the crime it did not commit? He talks of "guilt, atonement, more guilt." What does *that* mean? At the time of his father's death, Oskar abandons his drama and "grows up," albeit to become a four-foot-one hunchback. If I had to guess, I would say that Oskar embodies the leftist view of German atonement and growth after the war—a misshapen growth that for some reason the rest of the world regarded as the West German miracle.

Perhaps I am, after all, the ugly American, for I find in some of this what I would call the intentional obscurity, which Tom Wolfe so detests, found, for example, in the writing of Umberto Eco. One's ear listening to the words always harkens back to Proust, but Proust always points in a direction. One feels like there is nothing gratuitous in Proust; everything is there for a reason. In *The Tin Drum* there is the feel of the author showing off, that he can spin a yarn simply for its own sake, but he comes to a dead end.

By comparison, it is easy to think of Gabriel García Márquez and *One Hundred Years of Solitude* or even any of Mark Helprin's novels, such as *Winter's Tale* or *A Soldier of the Great War.* Each of these leaves the reader with feelings of loss and triumph. Grass, for all the dazzling work of a writer, leaves you with nothing.

24 October 2006

Voltaire in Love by Nancy Mitford

Fairly early in this book Nancy Mitford quotes her subject as saying about writing history, "If you want to bore the reader, tell him everything." This book, which only covers the years of Voltaire's life spent as the lover of Émilie, the Marquise du Châtelet, roughly 1733 to 1749, is most assuredly not a bore. Although it does not have the moments of laugh-out-loud humor of *The Pursuit of Love* or *Love in a Cold Climate*, it maintains the same light touch and sensibility of her fiction.

My first real encounter with Voltaire (other than that wretched, hackneyed epigram that everyone loves to quote) was Will and Ariel Durant's *Age of Voltaire*, which came out roughly 10 years after Mitford's book and which I read shortly thereafter while I was in high school. My recollections of that are fuzzy, but in recalling it and the volume that followed, *Rousseau and Revolution*, I have a (probably unjustified) memory of the Durants balancing Rousseau as the ultimate idealist of the Enlightenment and Voltaire as the ultimate cynic. Two things were clear: Rousseau was not a nice man and Voltaire was great fun (at least as much fun as a hypochondriac could be). The other thing that seems clear to me now is that Rousseau was one of the great jackasses of intellectual history.

Rousseau is mentioned only briefly in this book. What we are given is a sparkling narrative of an enchanted relationship in a time when such love affairs were the norm. The only difference in this one was the intellectual companionability of the couple. Émilie was, at a time when women received no education, a master of mathematics and eager to translate Sir Isaac Newton into French, which she ultimately did. Their relationship was physical for roughly half their years together. Voltaire declared himself unable to perform, then promptly began an affair with Madame Denis, his niece, which lasted the rest of his life. Miss Mitford notes that there was a papal dispensation in France as to marrying one's niece, so presumably affairs were okay, too. It may also explain why, the first time I dined at 21 in New York, the young women I saw dining with older executives were referred to as "nieces."

Roughly 38 years ago, as I was struggling to read all of Will and Ariel Durant's *The Story of Civilization*, I was specifically trying to read *The Age of Voltaire*. In reading this book, I did not remember much, if any, discussion of Émilie, so I took the volume off the shelf to see if my memory was correct.

Although there are numerous entries for the Marquise du Châtelet (which is mysteriously listed in the index under du) the Durants do not seem to put much emphasis on Voltaire's relationship with her as a defining influence. Miss Mitford's book is listed in the Durant's bibliography, and this treatment is, I suppose, simply evidence of the utter subjectivity of the interpretation of the historical record.

Perhaps the significance is the dichotomy of two basic views of history: one that sees it as the movement of ideas and the other (most emphatically urged on us by Thomas Carlyle) as the movement of great men. It is no accident, I think, that Miss Mitford includes in the frontispiece a quote from Carlyle. Clearly, she is more interested in the people than the ideas, not really explaining how thought, for this pair of philosophers (as they are always referred to), went from Cartesian to Newtonian. She does give us a vivid picture of the delight of that century, of Voltaire's sensibility, and of his undoubted deep and abiding love for this woman, even after she had become pregnant at the age of almost 40 by the rather caddish Marquis de Saint-Lambert. It was in fact, bearing his child that caused her death, which is tragic. But before this tragic denouement there is the high humor of the Marquise seducing her long-neglected husband so that he would believe the child was his. That is not so different, is it, from the ending of The *Pursuit of Love* in which Linda dies in childbirth with her French lover's child (he, a hero of the resistance, is shot by the Gestapo) and the true hilarity that precedes the tragedy? She was of a piece with Waugh's comment (on the back cover) that Mitford, having voted Socialist and done her best to make England unlivable, had gone to live in France.

15 November 2006

Reflections on the Revolution in France by Edmund Burke

Edmund Burke's most famous quote is somewhat less trite than Voltaire's most famous quote. Burke's (which I believe the late Howard K. Smith used in reporting from Alabama or Mississippi in the early 1960s) was to the effect that all that is required for evil to succeed is for good men to do nothing. In school as Americans we learn about Burke, the Whig member of Parliament, who supported the American colonies' war for independence. Later, I learned he was an essayist of the time and of the rank of Addison, Steele, and Dr. Johnson.

And then there is this book, which defines what George Will would refer to as a "Tory notion," and yet Burke was a conservative Whig. The terms, the names, the badges are long past fighting over. Rather, I think Burke is a bridge between the classical, ordered world and the modern world bifurcated into free and totalitarian that is described by Karl Popper, Hannah Arendt, and Eric Hoffer. His reflections are written in the form of a long letter, and in tone are almost apologetic for being judgmental.

Voltaire once wrote that people who believe in absurdities will eventually commit atrocities, and that was the sum and substance of Burke's view of the French Revolution. This is all the more prescient because it was written in 1790 before the execution of Louis XVI and before the ascent of the Jacobins over the Girondists, the formation of the Committee on Public Safety, and the commencement of the Reign of Terror.

Up until the events of 1789, the word "revolution" had a favorable connotation in English. Burke traces the constitutional rights of Englishmen not to the Magna Carta or the English Civil War, but to the Glorious Revolution of 1688. This is strangely balanced by his decrying of the confiscation of church property in

France. Because of his Irish connection and the fact that his mother was a Roman Catholic, Burke was always treated with suspicion, even in conservative Whig circles. But his reference to 1688 is, I think, consistent with his stated view that "a state without the means of some change is without the means of its conservation."

What this is, I believe, is the first straightforward denunciation of totalitarianism, which universally begins with the tyranny of the mob. And Burke is clearly not a believer in majority rule or one man, one vote. He writes the following:

I readily admit (indeed I should lay it down as a fundamental principle) that in a republican government, which has a democratic basis, the rich do require additional above what is necessary in monarchies. They are subject to envy and through envy, oppression.

Although one can hear the sniffing aristocrat in that pronouncement, it is also the best formulation explaining the ultimate dangers inherit in economic populism. He goes on to tell us that the "Rights of Man" were in fact an offensive weapon for confiscation, which harkens back 14 years to Jefferson's changing John Locke's expression "life, liberty, and property" to "life, liberty, and the pursuit of happiness."

Most of his argument on revenue and debt loses me, although I think what I glean is first and foremost an argument against paper money without backing. Clearly, he envisions a state with far more involvement in our lives than the free-trade and liberal economists of the 19th century would like.

What Burke provides is a brief for the same open society that Karl Popper and Hannah Arendt would explicate 150 years later. Burke's is the adumbration of a belief in the institutions of freedom as they devolved from the Magna Carta to the Glorious Revolution and the American Revolution as opposed to the imposition of one man's or group of men's all-encompassing theory of government. Perhaps his simple message is "God save us from the theorists."

12 December 2006

Speak, Memory by Vladamir Nabokov

If there is a single word to describe Nabokov, I think the word is *sly*.

In my sophomore year of college we read *Lolita* as part of a course on the contemporary novel. I was lucky on two counts: I was able to check the book out of the library rather than buying it (because I worked in the library, I was immune from overdue fines), and the volume I happened to check out was, in fact, the annotated *Lolita*. I had the advantage that the other dozen people in that class did not, of knowing that in addition to the humor, everything, and I mean everything, was a sly reference to something else.

And so we come to this book, originally written fairly early in Nabokov's career as a writer in English. It was then revised into its present form in the 1960s.

Although Nabokov did not come from a noble family, his family lived on a scale that would seem to equate to any English milord of the early 20th century. He writes of the 50 of so servants who saw to his family's comfort in both the house in St. Petersburg and on their country estate, as well as served the traveling entourage on regular trips to the south of France. It is Nabokov's ease with wealth; the fact that his father was an ardent promoter of freedom in Russia but categorically not a socialist; and the existence of French governesses, English tutors, and all manner of educational help and benefits that make one think of the smart-ass rich kid who is only saved from himself by the fact that he is smart, very smart. In this regard, I am given to think of the young American writer Michael Lewis, and that is only perhaps because I know Mr. Lewis's father and infer too much.

In the recollections of *Speak, Memory*, most of them of an

idyllic time and place, there is still the sly Nabokov, seeing the world as it is and also seeing the world as a hilarious absurdity. Much has been made of Nabokov's ability to remember minute detail from his childhood. Certainly the detail is there, but we have to be cautious, I think, because he could just as easily be pulling the reader's leg. This point is illustrated by an exchange I remember reading in Sam Tanenhaus's biography of Whittaker Chambers:

Garry Wills, who poured forth voluminous copy [at the *National Review*] while doing graduate work in classics at Yale, remembered Chambers participating in an excited discussion of a new literary sensation, Vladimir Nabokov's *Lolita*. "I was pushing the Poe references, Jim Burnham, *The Grand Guignol*," Wills recalled, while Chambers insisted, "It's just a funny book."

Nabokov does digress from time to time to tell us how he really feels about certain things, the first and foremost being that in the pantheon of monsters in the 20th century, Lenin is as bad as Stalin, and without Lenin there could not have been a Stalin. He also tells us much about the so-called psychological insights of some writers when he refers to Freud as "the Viennese quack."

Of his time in exile, which includes his years at Cambridge and his subsequent life in Berlin and France until he immigrated to the United States in 1940, he maintains his mask of detachment. He writes at one point of another Russian emigre writer in Berlin in the 1920s: "I developed a great liking for this bitter man, wrought of irony and metallic-like genius."

He could have been writing about himself.

30 December 2006

Malraux: A Life by Olivier Todd

Malraux comes to my mind as two dim recollections, one from childhood and the other a bit later. First, of course, he was the French official who escorted Jacqueline Kennedy around Paris. Later, in my teenage consciousness, he was one of the names that pseudointellectuals and poseurs of every stripe liked to drop, along with those of Jacques Barzun, Sartre, Camus, Jean-Jacques Servan-Schreiber, and perhaps John Kenneth Galbraith, to show that they were among the cognoscenti. These were people who generally never mentioned such names as Edmund Wilson or Isaiah Berlin, oddly enough.

This book, which is a thorough and seemingly honest biography, raises a question not often addressed—the role of the public intellectual. That is a debate from the past, the days when television supported a certain amount of ponderous discourse, the likes of David Suskind, William F. Buckley, Jr., or even Eric Sevareid talking to the likes of Galbraith or Arthur Schlesinger. That, of course, has now been replaced by the shout fests of *Crossfire, Hannity and Colmes*, and *Hardball with Chris Matthews*.

Malraux comes to us from an even more distant past. Despite his intellectual bona fides, Malraux was not in this most brass hat of societies, a graduate of the École Normale Supérieure, but was for the most part self-educated. Early on, he lived a life of the literary flaneur, journalist, and landmark looter in French Indochina. It is instructive to watch his career after his return to France in parallel with Hemingway's.

Both Hemingway and Malraux rallied to the aid of republican Spain in 1936. More than Hemingway (and I believe this even after reading Stephen Koch's book), he played along with and apologized for the Stalinists. Malraux visited the Soviet Union, knew Pasternak, met Gorky, and was far more a man of the Left. Hemingway viewed himself (if he could get beyond his ego) as an antifascist. Hemingway covered the Second World War as a correspondent; Malraux laid low in the south of France after the fall and really only joined the resistance after his two half brothers were carted away by the Gestapo. Like Hemingway, this fact did not prevent him from embellishing his involvement to the point of outright fabrication.

Because of Malraux's role as a public intellectual, Olivier Todd devotes minimal space to anything resembling analysis of Malraux's literary output. Malraux himself believed he was more deserving of the Nobel Prize than Hemingway or Faulkner was.

His transformation from a moderately well-known writer to an important public figure occurred in his association with Charles de Gaulle immediately after the war. It is easy to see Malraux's influence on de Gaulle as equal parts sycophant and hagiographer. I think that is too simple. It is easy to forget the utter mess of things that the Fourth Republic became, verging as it did through the early 1950s between a civil war pitting the Communists against the Right, or in its turn, those who wanted to leave Algeria with those who wanted to stay. In de Gaulle's virtual coup d'état in the spring of 1958, he needed the likes of Malraux not only for the lesser purposes if salving his ego but also for the clearly higher purpose of keeping the country from falling into chaos.

Malraux remained a Gaullist minister from then on, characterizing himself as the "Gaullist man of the left." It is the lesson of history that the characterizations of left and right will ultimately become meaningless. The dichotomy is between those who believe in freedom and those who do not. Malraux clearly did so believe, and just as clearly (in spite of the vaporings in his writing about the importance of the individual as an existentialist formulation), Sartre did not. Malraux will matter in 100 years for the same reason Orwell or Burke or Karl Popper will matter. The forces of freedom versus the forces of servitude will always remain in conflict as long as man is man.

22 December 2006

Les Liaisons Dangereuses by Choderlos de Laclos

It would seem to be extremely difficult to maintain the narrative flow of a story in an epistolary novel such as this, even more difficult than the use of many narrators. But the form is perfectly suited to the author's purpose, which is to depict the descent into complete moral depravity.

This book was a scandal when it was published in 1782, and one suspects it was considered something of a cross between *Lolita* and the *Kinsey Reports*. It was ignored for more than a century after the French Revolution, and in the last 30 years has been made into a play and at least three movies (two in English and one in French).

I suppose that a feminist critique of the work would be very damning, for our two main correspondents, the Vicomte de Valmont and the Marquise de Merteuil are both the very embodiment of evil. Yet, in the end, Valmont redeems himself to some extent, while the Marquise is unrepentant and, accordingly, is struck by something worse than the mark of Cain.

Valmont and the Marquise had been lovers. She is a widow, and he is something of a cad and a playboy. He wishes to seduce the virtuous Madame de Tourvel; she wishes to see her friend Madame de Volange's daughter, Cecile, seduced by the Chevalier Danceny, but also despoiled by Valmont first. All of this is sport to the two of them. In the process everyone's life is ruined: After her seduction, Madame de Tourvel flees to a convent where she dies of shame, Cecile de Volanges enters a convent, Danceny kills Valmont in a duel, and the Marquise is disfigured by small pox.

Is this a highly moral tale, or at least one with a highly moral ending? Not really, for up until the tragic denouement, everyone seems to be having a high old time. One wonders if

Laclos was not the immediate predecessor of the Marquis de Sade, who thought he could make a work publishable simply by giving it a moral ending. That is one way of looking at it. The other, which is not incompatible, is that it is a deep and occasionally moving insight into the way people who are utterly self-obsessed think.

Here is where the feminist critique comes into play. There is not a single motive, word, act, or gesture of the Marquise that does not have its origin in something truly evil. Is this borne of her (somewhat evident) desire to have Valmont back as her lover? How can that be? She is sleeping with Danceny, and no relationship seems to mean much of anything to her other than the opportunity to set that person up for a fall. Does she want Valmont back because he is her one true love or because that is the ultimate opportunity for revenge?

By contrast, Valmont almost welcomes his death at the hand of the cuckolded Danceny. The Marquise gets fate's revenge, and we are almost glad. Truth be told, there is no sympathetic character here. The good are too good and the evil, too evil. We are all somewhere between.

31 December 2006

Afterword
The Consolation of Books

Looking back at what I have put down here, I am not certain whether I have answered the question I set for myself—the question set by this project, but more significant, by the task of preparing reading lists year after year for more than a decade. The question, of course, is to what end should an individual's daily reading be put? Earlier, I most likely offended people who read simply to keep themselves entertained. That is wrong, if that is what I have done.

The reason it is wrong is because there is no such thing as mere entertainment, just bad or better bets on what is going to last. Both Dickens and Thackery provided mere entertainment in the *Cornhill Magazine*. Yet, at the same time, I am as convinced now as I was at the beginning of this exercise of the importance of Mr. McCall's comment to me nearly two decades ago, "But there are so many books I have not yet read." It is much easier to look back to find those books than to look on the current best-seller list. In addition, in a single lifetime of reading, it is impossible to say that one has read all of the old stuff that matters.

Another trepidation that sneaks up on me as I review these comments is that what I have written is actually a set of eighth-grade (or, I hope at least eighth grade) book reports, recalling that the purpose of those was to convince the teacher that one may have actually read selected parts of the book. My intent here was to record my reaction to what I read and not let it slip off into the ether. To the extent that I have accomplished this, I find it very satisfying. Yet, the book report part is frustrating, because most of the time as I look back over my recollections, I find myself saying, "That is not quite what I meant." That comes up almost as often as "how trite" or "how silly," or worse, "how pretentious."

Another objective, not quite met, was to record my thought entirely as a reaction to a book and not as a research project. On numerous occasions, I yielded to the temptation to pull another book off the shelf or check something online. This doubtless has the effect of degrading my effort from an intentionally unresearched book (for which fact checkers are unnecessary) to the lesser status of a poorly researched one.

Close to this bone is a wonderful book called *Footfalls in Memory* by Terry Waite, who was the Archbishop of Canterbury's special envoy to the Middle East and who was held captive, in virtual isolation, by Islamic militants in Lebanon, for five years. In that book (which takes its title from the *Burnt Norton* section of T. S. Eliot's *Four Quartets*) he relates how, as a captive, he maintained his sanity by revisiting the important books of his life. One can argue that every day is a minor task of preserving one's sanity. Moreover, books create our world both real and archetypal.

Our house in Baton Rouge, where the predominant part of my books are kept is referred to by my wife as "*The Library of Congress*" and those kept at the flat in Houston as "*The Library of Congress Annex*." It is true that I have purchased more books, and continue to purchase more books, than I will be able to read in my lifetime. Nevertheless, I take comfort in the fact that in the event of a nuclear or ecological holocaust that if isolated in either location for months at a time (I have long since given up on a blizzard doing something similar), I would have the means at hand that Terry Waite so courageously had to call up from deep within himself.

One reaches an age, I suppose, when the past becomes arcadian, and the view forward is one of sad desperation. Despite that truism, and the fact that civilization seems somehow to survive, and people (at least in the so-called industrialized nations) lead lives of better health and prosperity, there is something of a loss. It is, for America or perhaps the West, the same kind of loss celebrated by the Twelve Southerners in *I'll Take My Stand*.

My earliest memories include, at the age of 9, being allowed to stay up to watch Jack Paar. Paar had inherited the *Tonight Show* from its founder, Steve Allen. The idea of the show, as Paar said years later, was to create the illusion of eavesdropping on interesting people chatting quietly in a bar after the Broadway theaters had closed, exchanging witty and interesting stories. Hence, the original idea was not to have people on merely for the purpose of plugging something. That is why Paar could play up someone like Oscar Levant or Peter Ustinov. And why later with Merv Griffin's show we got to hear about London Music Hall life at the turn of the 20th century from Hermione Gingold. All of these people, to borrow J.D. Salinger's description of John Barrymore in *Franny and Zooey*, were "bright as hell and full of lore" without being "burdened down by any of the cumbersome luggage of a too formal education."

For people like Peter Ustinov and Oscar Levant or Frank Muir or Fred Allen or Henry Morgan (the *I've Got a Secret* panelist, not Colonel Potter from *M*A*S*H*) to hold forth the way they did, they must have read constantly and omnivorously. There is no reason to believe, for example, that David Niven had a publicist who used a focus group to come up with the title of his first volume of memoirs *The Moon's a Balloon*. He had doubtless read the e.e. cummings's poem that begins "who knows if the moon's a balloon" and ends with "and everyone's in love and flowers pick themselves."

One of my favorite catch phrases comes from those days. Merv Griffin was interviewing the veteran character actor Hans

Conreid, who described a particularly embarrassing moment in his career as allowing him to "resilver the mirror of humility."

By contrast, most of the literary knowledge of today's celebrities is, I think, pose. They can hire someone to give them the references, but they only engage in the silliest of exchanges on a show like *Letterman*. It is a sad fact that the kind of conversation that once upon a time took place on the *Tonight Show* or *Dick Cavett*, could not prosper on commercial television today. It is particularly sad because television is a medium ideally suited to including the audience in such witty conversation.

So perhaps, through books, it is conversation that I crave. That lost and greatly lamented commodity remains for me the elusive goal in all of this. There is a short list of people to whom I address not just this book, but real conversation.

A note on reading books in translation

When I was in college, I had a friend whom we referred to as "The Prince of Curacao." He came from a wealthy Dutch/Jewish family on that island where Dutch, Spanish, English, the local patois known as Pampiemento and several other languages co-exist. We used to joke that he was illiterate in five different languages. On many days I consider myself not to be fluent in several languages, including English, and I wonder if there is much value in reading translations of great works. This problem of the linguistic aspects of a work, is not simply style, ahead of more important consider-ations – theme, action and understanding of the human condition. Years ago we were told by Professor Rodolfo Batiza, who taught Latin American Law at Tulane, that translations were like women: "If they are faithful they are not beautiful, and if they are beautiful they are not faithful." Putting aside the sad fact that if he said that today in any institution of higher learning he would probably have a complaint lodged against him with some ombudsman some-where, the real problem is how are we to know? T.S. Eliot once wrote that Yeats was the greatest poet of his age in English and, insofar as he was able to judge, in any language. By this statement I think he was primarily putting Yeats ahead of Rilke and any number of French poets. Eliot was a polymath who was probably qualified to make such a judgment, yet I doubt that even he could appreciate nuance for nuance the beauty of a work in so many other languages. Of course, the fact is that he may have been refer-ring more to the scope of Yeats's achievement, which, by the lights of high modernism, was doubtless the greatest.

Francine Prose has recently pointed out that a work in translation is really a collaboration between the author and the translator—an obvious enough thing, and one can feel the difference between the last lines of Proust's *Le Temps Retrouve* in the Andreas Mayor translation and the Terence Kilmartin translation now issued by The Modern Library. Mayor's rendering of Proust's last line is probably less accurate and is unquestionably more beautiful, just as the whole of Scott Moncrieff's translation is. Scott Moncrieff's work takes its name from Shakespeare's Sonnet 30 rather than simply *In Search of Lost Time*. Perhaps it is not too late to seek a newer world and someday have a sense of the original.